ECONOMIC CORRIDOR DEVELOPMENT

FROM CONCEPTUAL FRAMEWORK TO PRACTICAL IMPLEMENTATION— GUIDANCE NOTE

SEPTEMBER 2023

ASIAN DEVELOPMENT BANK

ADB

© 2023 Asian Development Bank
6 ADB Avenue, Mandaluyong City, 1550 Metro Manila, Philippines
Tel +63 2 8632 4444; Fax +63 2 8636 2444
www.adb.org

Some rights reserved. Published in 2023.

ISBN 978-92-9270-318-9 (print); 978-92-9270-319-6 (electronic); 978-92-9270-320-2 (ebook)
Publication Stock No. TCS230348-2
DOI: http://dx.doi.org/10.22617/TCS230348-2

Note:
1. In this publication, "$" refers to United States dollars.
2. This guidance note is jointly prepared by the Central and West Asia Department (CWRD) and the Climate Change and Sustainable Development Department (CCSD) of the Asian Development Bank, with support from the Southeast Asia Department and the South Asia Department. Queries can be addressed to the Regional Cooperation and Integration Unit of CWRD, and the Regional Cooperation and Integration and Trade Division of CCSD.

Cover design by Edith Creus.

Contents

Appendixes

Tables, Figures, and Boxes

Abbreviations

ABEC	–	Almaty–Bishkek Economic Corridor
ADB	–	Asian Development Bank
CAREC	–	Central Asia Regional Economic Cooperation
CBTA	–	cross-border transport agreement
CCSD	–	Climate Change and Sustainable Development Department
CWRD	–	Central and West Asia Regional Department
DMC	–	developing member country
EARD	–	East Asia Regional Deparment
ECD	–	economic corridor development
ECP	–	Economic Corridor Program
ERDI	–	Economic Research and Development Impact
EWEC	–	East–West Economic Corridor
FAO	–	Food and Agriculture Organization of the United Nations
FEA	–	functional economic area
GMS	–	Greater Mekong Subregion
GDP	–	gross domestic product
GVC	–	global value chain
ICT	–	information and communication technology
IFI	–	international financial institution
km	–	kilometer
MFF	–	multitranche financing facility
MOU	–	memorandum of understanding
NOM	–	New Operating Model

NSEC	–	North–South Economic Corridor
OMDP	–	Office of Markets Development and Public–Private Partnership
OP7	–	ADB Strategy 2030 Operational Plan for Priority 7: Fostering Regional Cooperation and Integration, 2019–2024
PARD	–	Pacific Regional Department
PPP	–	public–private partnership
PRC	–	People's Republic of China
PSOD	–	Private Sector Operations Department
RC	–	Regional Cooperation and Operations Coordination Division
RCI	–	regional cooperation and integration
RCI-TG	–	RCI Thematic Group
RIBS	–	Regional Improvement of Border Services
RPG	–	regional public good
SARD	–	South Asia Regional Department
SASEC	–	South Asia Subregional Economic Cooperation
SEC	–	Southern Economic Corridor
SERD	–	Southeast Asia Regional Department
SEZ	–	special economic zone
SG	–	Sectors Group
SME	–	small and medium-sized enterprises
SG-FIN	–	Finance Sector Office
SPS	–	sanitary and phytosanitary
STKEC	–	Shymkent–Tashkent–Khujand Economic Corridor
TA	–	technical assistance
TTF	–	transport and trade facilitation

Executive Summary

The Asian Development Bank (ADB) included economic corridors into its regional cooperation and integration (RCI) operations almost a quarter century ago. ADB's RCI operations initially emphasized improving regional connectivity among its developing member countries (DMCs). Investments in transport infrastructure were soon complemented with "software" or policy and institutional components of RCI (e.g., coordination in border procedures and standards for trade and transport facilitation) to move goods across borders, facilitate access to raw materials, and promote integration into regional and global value chains.

This basic framework, centered on cross-border transport routes and transport and trade facilitation, has defined the development of economic corridors under ADB-supported subregional cooperation programs even if, conceptually, it was recognized that the development of economic corridors had a broader scope. The initial utility of this transport-centric approach to economic corridor development (ECD) has diminished considerably over 25 years of growth and changes in the Asia and Pacific region. The approach does not match the demands of DMCs for ECD and to best practices already in place in the Asia and Pacific region and beyond. The altered development context calls for a new and broader framework for ECD in ADB's RCI operations. In the past decade, ADB-supported subregional cooperation programs—the Greater Mekong Subregion (GMS) Program, the Central Asia Regional Economic Cooperation (CAREC) Program, and the South Asia Subregion Economic Cooperation (SASEC) Program—have started moving toward a more expanded approach to ECD. The actual implementation of the spatial approach has not been easy, and progress is varied, with little coordination across subregions.

This guidance note presents a new framework and operational guidelines to facilitate the emerging transition towards the broader approach to ECD. *Its starting point is recognizing ECD as a spatial or area-based concept—a process of widening, deepening, and integrating economic activities in an identified area through integrating the provision of diverse hard- and soft-infrastructure, sound economic incentives to attract private firms and investments, development of (new) markets, and strengthened institutions and regulations to support increased economic activities and density.*

The spatial approach rejects the prevalent and popular "butterfly model" of ECD, which assumes that providing a transport artery ("the caterpillar") will "transform it over time into an economic corridor" (i.e., "the butterfly"). In contrast, spatial ECD requires comprehensive visioning and planning at the outset for all intervention components and implementation phases. Infrastructure investments in ECD may encompass much more than just transport connectivity and include investments in human capital; policies and reforms to develop agriculture, manufacturing, and services sectors; and institutional components to address governance and public goods. Such multisector, multi-stakeholder-engaged ECD is more complex and challenging.

This guidance note provides a guide and reference tool for spatial ECD. The guidance note applies to all practitioners engaged in developing economic corridors, including government officials, development partners, the private sector, and academia in formulating, implementing, and assessing economic corridors.

Understanding the Complexities of Economic Corridor Development

There are four different ways of ECD in practice. The four approaches—transport corridors, trade corridors, regional development corridors, and spatial transformation corridors—rest upon reducing trading costs (including transportation) or exploiting various economies of agglomeration. The four categories of corridors can be loosely viewed as quasi-nested in that each is broader and more ambitious in scope than the preceding corridor approach. The classification into four categories of corridors is heuristic. It can be further refined into two broader classes of corridors: M-type for corridors focused on movement (transport and trade) and S-type for corridors whose starting unit is spatial (regional development, spatial transformation). This guidance note does not consider M-type corridors by themselves as economic corridors. They are regarded as necessary but not sufficient for ECD. ECD in this guidance note should therefore be understood as S-type corridors. Nonetheless, the guidance note refers to both M-type and S-type corridors, and the framework and operational guidelines developed can apply to both categories of corridors.

Rationale, Uses, and Benefits of Economic Corridor Development

The rationale for ECD combines the idea of unbalanced growth and uneven distribution of economic activities. Given limited resources and administrative capabilities, development processes should target areas and sectors with high potential to induce growth, including through backward- and forward-linkages. Unequal spatial distribution of economic activity reflects the "first and second nature" forces (physical geography and economic geography, respectively). These factors influence market-driven drivers of spatial growth, namely, agglomeration, specialization, and migration.

ECD can result in the development of corridor nodes (cities, towns), value chains at local and regional levels, greater local capture of value-added in the chains, and trade promotion. ECD planning can help DMCs address urbanization-related matters, such as urban migration. Successful ECD can bring diverse benefits for DMCs, such as (i) economic diversification, (ii) regional development and economic decentralization, (iii) entrepreneurship development, (iv) job creation and productivity growth, and (v) wide-ranging institutional development.

Economic Corridors in International Practice and ADB Operations

Three recent economic corridors are discussed, one in Africa and two in Asia, to contextualize the concepts and aspects in practice, such as development methodology and implementation on the ground. ECDs in ADB's RCI operations in ADB-supported GMS, CAREC, and SASEC subregional programs are also reviewed. The review spans from the narrow transport-centric focus of corridors in the early years to recent shifts toward spatial corridors started in 2012. The actual implementation of the spatial approach of ECD in the subregional programs has not been easy.

Framework for Economic Corridor Development

The new ECD framework consists of three phases: the first is a conceptual framework that encompasses the potentially wide scope of ECD interventions. Second is an operational framework that specifies what type of corridor makes sense in practical terms for ECD. And third are implementation guidelines to ensure that the planning and designing of a corridor meet the prerequisites for successful ECD. Important crosscutting issues in formulating ECD are also discussed along with potential pitfalls in implementation and criteria for assessing the success of ECD.

The conceptual framework outlines the underlying principles policymakers will generally assume in considering ECD. They include (i) the uniqueness of every ECD—avoiding "cut-and-paste" program design, (ii) the diverse structural and initial factors already in place, (iii) attributes suitable for ECD in the target area, and (iv) the complexity of ECD and the need for sophisticated technical analysis.

The operational framework categorizes economic corridors into four distinct zones in line with the corridor's level of scope and complexity: (i) domestic transport (or M-type) corridor, (ii) cross-border transport corridor, (iii) domestic spatial (or S-type) ECD, and (iv) cross-border spatial ECD. There is no presumption of normative ranking across the four ECD zones, and ADB may support its DMCs for all four categories. In terms of operations, what matters is identifying the suitable zone, specifying the starting point or zone, and mapping out the way forward right at the start of the ECD.

There are six stages in developing and implementing ECD:

(i)   conceptualizing the corridor and proof-of-concept—creating an overall ECD vision;

(ii)   initial stakeholder consultations leading to an early-stage memorandum of understanding;

(iii) conducting detailed strategic and feasibility study based on technical, economic, and additional analyses as needed;

(iv)   developing a masterplan—which includes a prioritized project pipeline, a formalized institutional structure for coordination and management, and resource mobilization;

(v)   specific project development, design, and implementation; and

(vi)   monitoring and evaluation.

Central to ECD is frequent, inclusive consultations with stakeholders—all levels of governments involved, development partners, the private sector, and civil society. Agreements with and among governments and agencies are critical for success. Plans for ECD need to be demand-driven to ensure government ownership.

Crosscutting issues discussed include the role of the public sector in ECD, political commitment and good governance over ECD and projects, and the need to ensure social inclusion and environmental sustainability. The role of the public sector and development finance institutions will be stronger during the early stages of ECD. The private sector's role will increase as public investments and other initiatives crowd in private capital and entrepreneurship. Even as ECD begins, some types of infrastructure, such as information and communications technology or urban infrastructure, are better handled through public–private partnerships (PPPs).

Well-functioning institutions and good governance are critical for negotiating the inevitable trade-offs that will sustain ECD over the long term. Mechanisms for transparency, wide participation, and accountability can offer predictability through the consistent application of rules, regulations, and laws of the countries involved.

Also, ECD planners and designers must work with vulnerable social groups to prevent any elite capture of corridor benefits. Similarly, careful monitoring of the environmental impact of projects must be included during the design stage to keep ECD as "green" as feasible.

Economic, social, and environmental indicators are essential tools for monitoring how well ECD is progressing at all levels during project implementation. Thus, systems for data collection should be established early.

Potential pitfalls that should be avoided include (i) ineffective institutions due to a weak corridor authority or poor design, (ii) vested interests and corruption, (iii) poor stakeholder coordination, (iv) lack of consensus among governments and agencies, and (v) issues over land acquisition and clearances. It is also important not to be overly optimistic when making assumptions or projections about resource mobilization, particularly from the private sector or for PPPs.

Mainstreaming Economic Corridor Development into ADB's Operations

ADB is transforming itself as it implements Strategy 2030 and its new operating model (NOM). ADB must adapt to retain its reputation as a leader in ECD as demand from DMCs for more S-type ECD grows.

ADB's strength for ECD starts with its expertise and experience in hard infrastructure projects. ADB-supported subregional programs show it does well in coordinating across countries, sectors, and stakeholders as an honest broker. ADB has a broad spectrum of financing options or instruments available for ECD. For example, technical assistance is important in the early stage of institutional coordination and analytical and technical preparatory work. Policy and institutional reform can be supported through program lending or results-based lending. ADB's sector-development program would apply where physical infrastructure investments must be combined with policy reform. Harnessing PPPs will be easier for national rather than cross-border projects, where ADB guarantees can help. In addition, ADB's private sector instruments will help private investment grow as ECD matures.

This guidance note suggests that a dedicated ECD team or unit be established with clear reporting lines, responsibilities, and accountability to ensure efficient multisector coordination for hardware and software projects. The composition of the ECD team, its skill mix, and potential locations within ADB are also discussed. Resident missions and finance divisions will have more important roles in ECD operations along with the RCI units in the regional department. Various other departments must work closely with regional departments to implement the new ECD framework. These include the Office of Markets Development and Public–Private Partnership (OMDP) and the Private Sector Operations Department (PSOD); knowledge groups such as Economic Research and Development Impact Department (ERDI), the Climate Change and Sustainable Development Department (CCSD) and the ADB Institute; along with relevant divisions within the new Sectors Group (SG) coordinated by the RCI Thematic Group.

1 Introduction

The Asian Development Bank (ADB) included economic corridor development (ECD) in its regional cooperation and integration (RCI) operations nearly a quarter century ago. ADB supported applying economic corridors as a tool to promote economic growth and wider economic benefits—starting with the Greater Mekong Subregion (GMS) Economic Cooperation Program in the 1990s.[1] Subsequently, ADB adopted economic corridors in its operations in the Central Asia Region Economic Cooperation (CAREC) Program and the South Asia Subregion Economic Cooperation (SASEC) Program.

RCI initially emphasized cross-border connectivity between ADB's developing member countries (DMCs) as a prerequisite to expand international trade, facilitate mobility, and deepen economic cooperation. Landlocked countries, in particular, required greater connectivity to enhance economic opportunities. But these investments in physical infrastructure needed the "software"—or policy and institutional components of RCI such as coordinated border procedures and standards to facilitate trade and transport—to move goods across borders, better access raw materials, and promote integration into regional and global value chains (GVCs).

This basic framework, centered on cross-border transport routes and trade facilitation—referred to here as the Economic Corridors Program (ECP)—defined corridor development under ADB-supported subregional cooperation programs even if conceptually it was recognized that they encompassed a much broader scope. For various reasons, using ECP as originally defined evolved considerably over 25 years, which have seen widespread economic growth and changes in DMC demand across Asia and the Pacific. This altered development context led to the need for a new and broader conceptual framework—an ECD approach—within ADB's RCI operations.

The first reason for an expanded ECP approach is its own past success. DMCs benefited greatly from the significant increase in cross-border connectivity resulting from the billions of dollars invested in transboundary transport routes under ADB-supported subregional cooperation programs.[2] Thus, demand for cross-border transport facilities has diminished—and the trend is expected to continue. Instead, DMCs are increasingly confronted with the urgent challenges of climate change, migration, urbanization, and economic diversification. The current ECP has little to offer in addressing these challenges.

---

[1] The GMS adopted the economic corridor approach at its Eighth GMS Ministerial Conference in Manila in 1998. ADB. 2018. *Review of the Configuration of the GMS Economic Corridors*. Manila.

[2] ADB. 2022. *Regional Cooperation and Integration Corporate Progress Report 2017–2020*. Manila.

Second, international trade and value chains have changed over time, with a diminishing share of primary exports, changes in relative percentages of intra- and inter-industry trade, and transformed services trade due to the application of new technologies (McKinsey 2019). This led DMCs to plan how to transform and upgrade their value chains to make them better fit the realities of today's international trading system and expected changes.

Third, the context for regional public goods (RPGs) in RCI has also changed over time. There is new demand for promoting digitalization while stemming cross-border financial crime and a new focus on issues such as reducing the cross-border spread of communicable diseases and tackling climate change. RCI must continue to adapt its tools to respond to the evolving context of providing effective RPGs.

Finally, expectations on the scope and use of economic corridors have changed significantly since the inception of the ECP. Economic corridors have been used widely across the globe in diverse settings, particularly the 21st century, with different scope and applied methodologies. The accumulated experience and lessons learned underline the inadequacy of the traditional ECP framework in helping DMCs address demand for developing economic corridors across Asia and the Pacific. These lessons apply within ADB and the subregional cooperation programs that have expanded their approaches of economic corridors over the past decade. These shifts are in the early stage, more evident at the strategic level, but are beginning to trickle down into operations and projects. Attempts to incorporate these shifts remain somewhat ad hoc and program- or region-specific, with little coordination across ADB.

This guidance note presents a new framework and operational guidelines to facilitate the transition toward **the new ECD approach, distinct from the previous ECP**. The new framework is inclusive, comprehensive, and more complex than the earlier focus on the linear infrastructure of regional transport routes and trade facilitation. Under this new framework, ECD is a spatial or area-based concept—a process of widening, deepening, and integrating economic activities in a spatially targeted area by integrating the provision of diverse "hard"- and "soft" infrastructure, sound economic incentives to attract private firms and investments, the development of (new) markets, and strengthened institutions and regulations to support increased economic activities and density. The direct outcome of ECD includes a region more competitive in attracting investments (including foreign direct investment), developing entrepreneurship, and attracting a skilled workforce.

One important aspect of this spatial approach is rejecting the **"butterfly model" of ECD**, which has been prevalent in the past and remains popular today. The model assumes that providing a transport artery (the caterpillar) will "transform it over time into an economic corridor" (the butterfly). In contrast, spatial ECD requires a comprehensive vision and plan at the outset for all components and implementation phases. ECD infrastructure investments move beyond transport connectivity to energy, urbanization, irrigation, and information and communications technology (ICT) investments. It includes other diverse components such as investments in human capital related to health, education, and skills; policies and reforms to develop agriculture, manufacturing, and services; and the institutional components that address governance and public goods. The multisector and multi-stakeholder ECD is more complex and challenging than the previous ECP.

This guidance note provides a helpful guide and reference tool for new ECD initiatives that are broader and more ambitious in scope. The guidance note applies to all practitioners engaged in developing economic corridors, including government officials, development partners, the private sector, and academia, in formulating, implementing, and assessing economic corridors. It is mainly directed to development agencies traditionally active in supporting ECD, which have also relied on the transport-centered ECP and have partnered with ADB in pursuit of their own RCI priorities. This new framework may contribute to a shared understanding toward next-generation ECD in promoting RCI. Such coordination among development partners would be essential for mobilizing the larger technical and financial resources needed for the ECD agenda ahead.[3] Researchers and academics working on improving ECD are another audience that may find this guidance note useful.

---

[3]   For example, the GMS program is currently formulating a new Regional Investment Framework with a pipeline of regional projects serving as a high-profile tool to interface with Developing Partners in mobilizing resources. A shared understanding on the new, expanded ECD framework could allow more GMS corridor projects to be supported, including those not typically falling under the previous, more narrowly focused ECP.

2 Understanding the Complexity of Economic Corridor Development

There is no standardized definition of ECD. ECD has been viewed from many different perspectives. This is because ECD overlaps with other topics such as economic geography, regional development, spatial planning, urbanization, agglomeration, clusters and transport networks, industrial development, along with regional and international trade. Each has its own history and underlying theories, which generates a wide, heterogeneous, and diffuse literature.[4] Given the operational focus of these guidelines, it is useful to consider the different ways ECD has been viewed in practice to consider how ADB might best use ECD in its operations. Four different approaches to corridor development can be identified: transport, trade, regional development, and spatial transformation.

In the context of spatial or area-based ECD, it is helpful to think of functional economic areas (FEAs)—as distinct from administratively defined areas such as towns, cities, or provinces.[5] Identification of FEAs assesses geographical areas in terms of trade links such as buying and selling industrial and consumer goods and services and labor. A FEA is defined as a geographical area comprising of a relatively self-contained and cohesive network of trade links (Box 1).

A conceptually useful starting point for an ECD is a **transport** corridor, which has both simple physical and functional characteristics. A transport corridor connects two or more nodes that may be economic clusters (or FEAs) of varying sizes, including endpoints that may be gateways to external regions. Their relative conceptual simplicity notwithstanding, transport corridors are found everywhere as they generally have a strong development impact.[6]

Some literature highlights the role transport corridors and logistic infrastructure play in connecting economic centers to promote trade and growth (Arnold 2005; Arvis, et al. 2011; Buiter and Rahbari 2011). These trade corridors may be domestic or, more often, regional, connecting regions covering two or more countries. Examples include the Maputo Corridor linking the Maputo port to industrial areas in eastern South Africa or the transport route connecting landlocked Bolivia with the Pacific Ocean or Nepal with the Bay of Bengal.

---

[4] For a relatively succinct overview that covers several areas linked to ECD, see Sugiyarto (2020). Brand (2017) provides more detailed and expansive coverage of literature linked to ECD.

[5] FEAs or regions are used in many economies for economic monitoring, modeling, and analytical purposes. The United States (US) Bureau of Economic Analysis, for example, divides the US economy into 172 FEAs. See US Department of Transportation. Final Redefinition of the BEA Economic Areas or bea. 2004. New BEA Economic Areas For 2004. News Release. 17 November.

[6] ADB et al. (2018). The impact goes well beyond the usual savings in time and vehicle-operating costs used in cost-benefit analysis to wide-ranging effects on land and labor markets and longer-term growth. Prominent examples in recent decades include the transport corridors in the PRC and the Golden Quadrilateral in India. For a different transport mode, Donaldson (2010) presents evidence of the strong growth impact of the extensive railway network in colonial India. For a meta-analysis of the quantitative impact of transport corridors, see Roberts et al. (2018).

> ### Box 1: Economic Corridor Development and Functional Economic Areas
>
> Functional economic areas (FEAs) are often identified using local and regional commuting for work, consumer shopping, and supply chain patterns (EMSI 2007). The concept of a "central place"—a settlement that provides certain goods and services (or "functions") to the surrounding area, an area defined by "market reach"—is also used. For example, small agricultural distribution towns may serve as a central "dominant" place for nearby rural areas. These towns are, in turn, dominated by "higher-order" central places like larger towns and cities, each offers more functions than the places it dominates. The hierarchy of nested places comprises an FEA. A related approach recently used by ADB defines a "natural city" as a contiguously illuminated area from satellite images of night-time lights.[a]
>
> A FEA can thus consist of several hierarchic entities or administrative areas such as a metropolitan center, adjacent towns, and rural communities. In areas of low population density, such as Central Asia, FEAs may be clearly demarcated and geographically separated. By contrast, they may overlap in more densely populated regions. Here, "area" refers to a FEA, and "region" may consist of two or more FEAs.
>
> Geographic scale also matters in a spatial context: Economic corridor development (ECD) can comprise different elements depending on its objectives and the scale of the geographical area. For example, an ECD may include mainly urban development and last-mile connectivity if it aims to develop a single FEA consisting of a city (node) and its adjoining hinterland. Alternatively, an ECD may incorporate regional development if the targeted FEA encompasses several administrative regions, cities of diverse sizes, and their adjacent communities. If the relevant scale comprises several FEAs, an ECD may include improved connectivity to reduce transport and other trade costs between FEAs. In other cases, the ECD may integrate two or more FEAs into a single, larger FEA for economies of scale and agglomeration (Figure 1).
>
> Source: NITI Aayog and Asian Development Bank. 2022. *Cities as Engines of Growth.*

A broader but similar version of ECD, mixing both transport and trade corridors, focuses on the role transport networks play (rather than an artery) in connecting geographical regions to promote the movement of goods and people (for domestic and international trade). For example, the early conceptualization of economic corridors in the 1990s by the European Union and GMS envisaged ECD as deepening transport infrastructure and networks to connect different regions.[7] This included cross-border trade as well as domestic economic integration, as the relevant operational regions in both instances spanned several economies. Other initiatives, such as the People's Republic of China's (PRC) Belt and Road Initiative and a new CAREC economic corridor—the Shymkent-Tashkent-Khujand Economic Corridor (STKEC)—also broadly conform to this ECD approach.[8]

A third ECD variant targets **regional development**. This approach differs from building on transport corridors by being area-based, identifying a geographical region, and promoting the development of the component of FEAs and their trade links with one another.[9] This may require transport infrastructure such as roads, rails, and ports, among others, and other interventions such as urban development,

---

7   See for example, ADB (2018) on GMS and Böttcher (2006) on TEN-T. The EU project had a wider scope, including multimodal and intermodal networks encompassing roads, railways, ports, inland waterways, and airports, as well as liberalization of transport markets

8   Sugiyarto (2019). The PRC's Belt and Road Initiative sometimes referred to as the New Silk Road, is an ambitious infrastructure program. Launched in 2013, it aims to establish a global footprint to significantly expand the PRC's economic and trade linkages. It includes six planned economic corridors: (i) PRC–Mongolia–Russian Federation Economic Corridor; (ii) New Eurasian Land Bridge; (iii) PRC–Central Asia–West Asia Economic Corridor; (iv) PRC–Indochina Peninsula Economic Corridor; (v) PRC–Pakistan Economic Corridor (CPEC); and (vi) Bangladesh-PRC-India-Myanmar Economic Corridor. STKEC is still in its early stages and may have other components, but it is likely to be transport dominated during its initial phase.

9   Transport networks would channel their growth impact by reducing trade costs and increasing inter-regional and international trade. Regional development would encompass developing FEAs within a targeted region and exploiting increased trade between regions derived from the lower trade costs.

special economic zones (SEZs) (including industrial parks and cross-border economic zones), and specific industrial policies for growth. Malaysia provides a good example of the regional development approach (section IV). Starting in the 1990s, Malaysia adopted ECD to address regional imbalances (across states and the rural–urban divide) and strengthen national growth quality. In addition to a corridor each in Sabah and Sarawak, three corridors were established in Peninsular Malaysia: the East Coast Economic Corridor, the Northern Corridor Economic Region, and the Iskandar Malaysia in South Johor. Each corridor focuses on different economic activities—agriculture, specific industries, renewable energy, and tourism, among others—with policies and resources focused on the selected economic and spatial targets (ADB 2014, Athukorala and Narayanan 2017). In the last decade, ADB also supported spatial/regional development projects under its RCI operations, such as a cross-border economic zone between the PRC and Viet Nam and India's Industrial Corridors. The regional development approach was also used in GMS initiatives through investments in the development of towns along GMS corridors.

Finally, the fourth ECD approach involves **spatial transformation**—capturing the agglomeration benefits and scale economies by integrating or merging independent FEAs to increase the density, range, and scope of economic activities. An example is CAREC's Almaty–Bishkek Economic Corridor (ABEC), which started in 2014. ABEC aims to integrate the cities and surrounding areas of Almaty in Kazakhstan, which has the highest economic density in Central Asia, and Bishkek, the capital city of the neighboring Kyrgyz Republic. While the 200-kilometer (km) ABEC links some transport investments to, for example, tourism, more initiatives focus on making the region a unified economic space for the health and education sectors, urban development, and disaster risk management. The PRC is an active proponent of urban agglomerations to reshape its own economic geography, with several large examples including the Beijing-Tianjin-Hebei Metropolitan Region ("Jing-Jin-Ji"), the Yangtze River Delta, and the Pearl River Delta.[10]

The literature and examples of economic corridors reiterate a key attribute underlying their heterogeneity: a corridor is intrinsically a spatial concept that also embodies movement across its space. The nature of the space under consideration varies across the different approaches to economic corridors. At one extreme, the space may be characterized as linear—a transport corridor or highway (national or regional). In other cases, it can be the immediate vicinity of the highway (picture a miles-long strip mall) or a wider space affected by the transport corridor. At a broader level, the starting point for an economic corridor is not any specific infrastructure asset but a spatial region,[11] in which the ECD consists of developing components of the subregions or hubs along with greater connectivity within the subregions or hubs. Alternatively, a space-based ECD may focus on integrating an identified region's subregions into an agglomerated and unified entity. Space-based ECDs may comprise, apart from individual road infrastructure, a wide spectrum of initiatives for infrastructure networks (roads, railways, ports, energy, ICT, and urban development, among others) along with systems and institutions (markets, policies, institutions, and governance).

The classification of economic corridors into four categories (anchored respectively on transport, trade, regional development, and spatial transformation) is heuristic. It can be further refined into two broader classes of corridors. The starting point and primary focus of the first two categories (transport and trade) is the movement of goods and people and can be considered "M-type" corridors.

---

[10]   Fang and Yu (2017). The PRC is building agglomerations to become global economic cores. It has proposed building a hierarchical urban agglomeration system with five large national urban agglomerations, nine regional- medium-sized urban agglomerations and six subregional smaller urban agglomerations.

[11]   A region comprises of two or more FEAs, and subregions as FEAs.

Similarly, the focus of the latter two categories is spatial and can be considered "S-type" corridors (Figure 1).

The blue circles in Figure 1 denote FEAs of various sizes, while the rectangular boxes represent regions

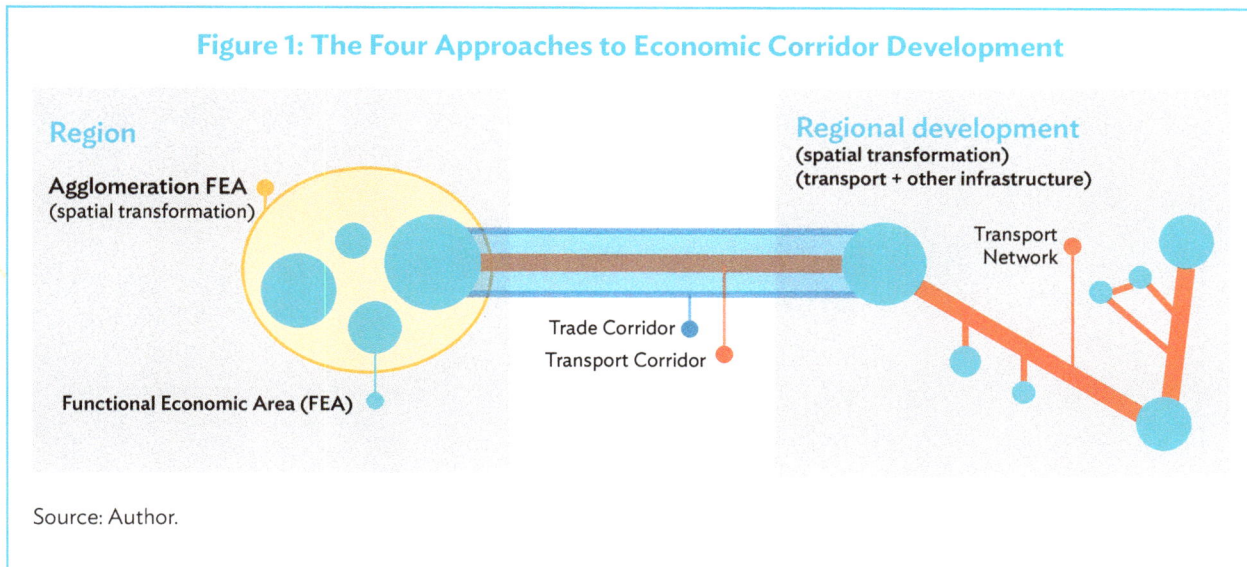

Figure 1: The Four Approaches to Economic Corridor Development

comprised of FEAs. A transport corridor connecting two FEAs in separate regions is a red line. A trade corridor is shown within the dashed lines, indicating the addition of logistics, warehousing, and other services, and trade facilitation for cross-border transport. A spatially transformative ECD is depicted in the "Region" box on the left by the yellow oval integrating four FEAs to benefit from the scale and agglomeration of a larger economic cluster. The "Regional Development" ECD on the right represents individual FEAs linked through diverse infrastructure investments and other regionally planned initiatives combined with enhanced connectivity between FEAs to reduce trade costs and increase intraregional trade.

The four ECD categories can be loosely viewed as quasi-nested in that each is broader and more ambitious than the preceding approach. For example, a trade corridor is difficult to implement without good transport corridors in place. Similarly, an ECD anchored on regional development or spatial transformation will have limited success without access to robust corridors enabling international or domestic trade. This underlying scaffolding of trade promotion for all four ECD categories explains why ECD has been and remains an important part of ADB's RCI operational toolkit.

As mentioned, this note does not consider M-type corridors as ECDs by themselves—they are necessary but not sufficient for an ECD. Here, ECDs are considered S-type corridors. Nonetheless, both M-type and S-type corridors are mentioned for two reasons. First, the framework and operational guidelines are inclusive and can apply to both categories. Second, the M-type and S-type categories are heuristically useful in understanding the earlier generation of ECD initiatives. In many of these cases, M-type corridors were viewed as the first stage of an ECD accompanied by an almost ritualized invocation that they would, over time, "transform into full-fledged economic corridors." Even where an ECD was clearly framed as spatial, the approach on the ground remained an M-type corridor.[12] Experience has made clear that time alone is not sufficient to transform M-type corridors into S-type corridors. And time has not been kind to the underlying notion that there are "stages of growth" in an ECD (from the "caterpillar" of a transport corridor to the "butterfly" of a spatial corridor. A successful ECD must be comprehensively planned from the start, even if the initial phases include M-type corridors. This guidance note provides an operational template for doing so.

---

[12]   This is discussed further in an ADB context in section V. It is not uncommon to conflate transport connectivity (M-type) dimensions with ECD in the recent literature (Isono and Kumagai 2020).

3 Rationale, Uses, and Benefits of Economic Corridor Development

The rationale for ECD rests on the idea of unbalanced growth and uneven distribution of economic resources and activities.[13] Unbalanced growth theory argues that with limited resources and administrative capabilities, development processes cannot be set in motion simultaneously for all sectors and regions of a country. It should be targeted in those sectors with high potential to induce growth—including through backward and forward linkages. ECD combines this idea with the empirical regularity of spatially unbalanced economic geography. As an economy moves beyond agriculture, where production is distributed relatively evenly across space, economic activities tend to concentrate unevenly in clusters or geographical pockets. A spatially targeted approach can also magnify the growth impact by improving coordination and synergies across various initiatives.

Unequal spatial distribution of economic activities is often explained in terms of "first and second nature" forces (Krugman 1993) that may sometimes complement or compete with each other. The first nature force refers to physical geographic characteristics, such as climate, coastal areas, rivers, mountain ranges, and agricultural land, among other natural endowments. The second nature force, by contrast, refers to economic geography or the spatial aspects of human activity, such as infrastructure assets that alter the costs of economic interaction among people, production, and services or institutions providing collective benefits. These factors together shape the "three market-driven drivers" of spatial growth: agglomeration economies, trade and specialization, and factor mobility or migration. In this context, ECD can be viewed as comprising collective public and private actions to change these three growth drivers to foster economic growth in specific locations.

Agglomeration economies induce firms to gravitate toward each other to form groups or clusters. They can benefit from agglomeration or external economies by reducing costs and fostering innovation. Co-location, for example, can broaden markets for suppliers that reduce costs through economies of scale. Suppliers can also provide inputs customized to the need of specific firms. Similarly, workers are attracted to places with an array of potential employers that allow firms better to match labor skills with their customized production needs. The concentration of firms and workers also facilitates learning from each other, and knowledge spillover can happen both within and across industries (World Bank 2009).

Trade and specialization forces people, regions, and countries to specialize in producing certain goods and services where they hold an advantage. Greater specialization, in turn, allows them to benefit from economies of scale that further expand their trade advantage. This leads to uneven distribution of economic activities and growth that, in turn, leads to migration, driven by the desire to seek better opportunities for personal advancement. The inflow of migrants increases population

---

[13] Unbalanced growth and "big push" as development strategies were introduced following the end of the Second World War by Albert Hirschman and others, such as Hans Singer and Paul Streeten.

density, generates externalities, and stimulates growth, which in turn makes migration more attractive. Migration occurs on three geographic scales: from rural to urban areas, between lagging and leading regions within a country, and between countries (FAO 2014).

The central question for any ECD is, therefore, how to use these three driving forces to stimulate economic density and boost economic competitiveness in certain locations. If governments can influence the location decision of firms and workers using proactive ECD investments and public strategies, they can increase economic density, competitiveness, and growth in a targeted economic space.

Critical factors affecting the location decisions of private firms to invest include, at a minimum, access to markets, raw materials, good infrastructure (transport, energy, ICT, urban infrastructure), and a safe, predictable, and business-friendly environment. Investments and policies to address these factors are at the core of a well-designed ECD.

Given the uneven distribution of economic activities, ECDs will typically focus on developing and connecting nodes where economic activities are concentrated, such as in large and second-tier urban centers and market towns in FEAs. These nodes serve to attract clusters and hubs of producers to increase their density and specialization. The corridor's nodes thus benefit from infrastructure investments and complementary policies and regulations that enhance their competitiveness.

Connecting the firms in ECD nodes to markets and raw materials helps develop national, regional, and GVCs. The value chains can link economic agents in the peripheries of the targeted areas to those in the more developed nodes or link the ECD to international consumers and sellers as part of the global production networks and/or GVCs.

Two important uses of ECDs follow directly from their role in value chains and nodal (urban) development: promoting RCI and managing urbanization. Increased access to markets and raw materials requires fast and cheap movement of goods (as well as factors of production) across the ECD. If the region includes sovereign boundaries, then trade facilitation, cross-border logistics, policy coordination, and other aspects of RCI become a priority. Economic corridors have a major role to play in RCI, whether connecting landlocked countries to international markets and, equally, connecting other countries to raw materials and cheaper labor. Cross-border ECDs also provide a platform for countries to effectively manage the provision of RPGs. Spatially-based ECDs can improve social services (education and primary health) in border areas (Srivastava 2016).

ECDs can help DMCs address another major challenge: rapid and large-scale urbanization. This has already led to unplanned urban sprawl that leads to low-productivity jobs, increased vulnerability of marginalized groups, and negative environmental impact. A well-designed ECD can help countries plan how to restructure their spatial economic geography to prevent or mitigate these negative effects of urbanization. This can include the planned expansion of existing large urban centers as well as the creation of second- and third-tier towns or greenfield developments that better manage rural–urban migration. In a related but separate context, it is increasingly recognized that growth in most modern economies is largely explained by urban expansion and that "getting cities right" is one of the best strategies for developing economies. ECDs can be a valuable and focused instrument for meeting that objective.

Successful ECDs can have diverse benefits, including (i) economic diversification; (ii) regional development and economic decentralization; (iii) enhanced competitiveness through deeper and wider domestic, regional, and GVCs; (iv) entrepreneurship development; (v) job creation and productivity growth; and (vi) wide-ranging institutional development (a certain amount is a prerequisite for a successful ECD). These benefits, combined, can bring long-term benefits to socioeconomic growth.

Targeted infrastructure development focused on the spatially oriented impact of sectoral policies can help diversify an economy. Sector-focused economic corridors (for example, in agro-industries, biotech, ICT, or tourism) can help countries promote or further develop their comparative advantage internationally or establish new industries as drivers of future growth. Similarly, ECDs can support regional diversification within countries by boosting existing corridor nodes to amplify new growth poles or by establishing new growth nodes. Increased spatial integration within an ECD project can thus enhance growth in new regions leading to geographical decentralization.

Increased economic density in ECD nodes can help countries increase their value-added within existing value chains. The agglomeration and economies of scale fostered by ECDs can help local businesses integrate into regional and GVCs, creating new niches or deepening existing opportunities by maximizing comparative advantage. The ECD's dynamic ecosystem allows more opportunities for entrepreneurs to innovate in existing or new lines of business that create more good jobs as worker productivity grows. This, in turn, attracts more skilled workers into the ECD and incentivizes other workers to acquire new knowledge and learn new skills.

ECDs also support institutional development. They require the participation of a variety of sectors and stakeholders, including government agencies at the national, provincial, and local levels. They must find new ways to manage the complex ECD and attract private firms and investments by strengthening collaboration between the public and private sectors. ECDs can also be catalytic in strengthening laws and regulations, especially to enhance an environment where public–private partnerships (PPPs) can thrive. Social mechanisms for coordination and interface between the government and other actors, such as civil society, political groups, and socially disadvantaged groups, are also needed in the process. Finally, to the extent that ECDs require high levels of governance in transparency, accountability, and inclusiveness (of public and private institutions), society as a whole will reap substantial benefits over the long term.

4 Economic Corridors in International Practice

This chapter provides selected examples of recent economic corridors to contextualize the ideas discussed so far. There is no shortage of examples, as many corridors have been developed worldwide over the past 3 decades. Economic corridors have been established in Africa, Latin America, and Asia, as well as in many Organisation for Economic Co-operation and Development countries as "growth corridors." The examples highlight ECD concepts and important practical aspects, including development methodology and on the ground implementation. They are representative as they share some common features. The first example is from Africa—where corridors have proliferated since 2000—and is primarily an M-type regional corridor. The other two examples are S-type corridors in Asia.

Northern Corridor Initiative, Eastern Africa

The Northern Corridor Initiative links landlocked countries in the Great Lakes Region of Eastern Africa—Burundi, Democratic Republic of Congo, Rwanda, Uganda, and South Sudan—to the gateway maritime port of Mombasa in Kenya. It is a multimodal trade corridor consisting of roads and railways in Kenya and Uganda, along with inland waterways on the Congo and Nile rivers and Kivu, Albert, and Victoria lakes.[14] In addition to transport investments, the corridor has significant trade and transport facilitation components. These were formalized in the Northern Corridor Transit and Transport Agreement, originally signed in 1985 but revised in 2007.

The revised agreement is quite comprehensive, defining 11 protocols on strategic areas for RCI:

(i)   Maritime Port Facilities;
(ii)   Routes and Facilities;
(iii)   Customs Controls and Operations;
(iv)   Documentation and Procedures; (v) Transport of Goods by Rail;
(v)   Transport of Goods by Road;
(vi)   Inland Waterways Transport of Goods;
(vii) Transport by Pipeline;
(viii) Multimodal Transport of Goods;
(ix)   Handling of Dangerous Goods; and
(x)   Measures of Facilitation for Transit Agencies, Traders, and Employees.

---

[14]   In practice, less than 4% of goods leaving Mombasa port traveled by rail in 2015. Railway networks, until recently, were inefficient, with poor maintenance and limited capacity to transport goods. Countries included in the corridor have since promoted railway development using Standard Gauge Railways.

The corridor is managed by the supranational Northern Corridor Transit and Transport Coordination Authority, which was "established and mandated by the Member States to oversee the implementation of the agreement, monitor its performance, and *transform the Northern trade route into an economic corridor*."[15] The authority includes a Council of Ministers for Transport, a secretariat located in Mombasa, and an executive board consisting of an intergovernmental committee of senior officials. For 2021–2022, the secretariat's budget was $4.4 million.[16]

There has been significant progress in upgrading roads, resulting in reduced transport costs and travel times. Under the transport and trade facilitation agreement, countries are working to improve border-crossing facilities, introduce one-stop border posts, replace multiple customs verifications with a joint verification, eliminate differences in customs laws and instruments, as well as road, police and customs roadblocks by, for example, replacing multiple weighing stations with high-speed weigh-in-motion systems.

The Northern Corridor enjoys high-level political commitment from all countries involved—partly reflecting their landlocked geography—and is supported by external development partners. Despite progress made thus far, several challenges remain. Port inefficiencies delay the release of goods. A large proportion of trucks that ply the trade routes are overweight due to incorrect official declarations. Multiple unproductive stops must be made to comply with "non-tariff barriers." Aside from the unofficial payments, they all increase transit times. The one-stop border posts suffer from poor implementation and continue to delay border crossings given unsynchronized working hours due to different time zones.

Economic Corridor Development in Malaysia

Malaysia is a multi-ethnic federation of 13 states and 3 Federal Territories. The government emphasized balanced regional development from early on in its development planning.[17] Six regional development authorities were set up in the 1970s for the northern, eastern, southern, and central regions, as well as for Sabah and Sarawak. These created extended road networks and new towns and developed remote areas to reduce poverty and regional disparities. Starting with its 9th Five-Year Plan in 2006–2010, Malaysia shifted its strategy by establishing five economic corridors to further address continued regional imbalances while pushing for broad economic growth.

The ECD strategy emphasized an increasing role of the private sector to drive regional growth and move up its value chains to a more knowledge-based economy. Customized masterplans were developed for each corridor in consultation with the private sector and other stakeholders. Each ECD plan had common features of identifying specific priority sectors, and building a conducive business environment to attract large investors as corridor anchors along with other private investors.

The parliament established a corridor implementation authority for each corridor, including the prime minister or deputy prime minister and the chief minister of participating states. Their mandate is to set strategy, policy, direction, and initiative to develop the corridors and implement their respective master plans. They are also responsible for attracting and working with private investors, managing stakeholder

---

[15]   Italics added. South Sudan acceded to the protocols in 2012.
[16]   The East African. 2021. Northern Corridor gets $4.4m for trade projects. 17 August.
[17]   See presentations by Malaysia's Economic Planning Unit and PEMANDU at the CAREC-IMT-GT workshop on economic corridors in Kuala Lumpur (https://www.carecprogram.org/?event=workshop-economic-corridor-development-apr-2014). This section also draws on ADB (2014) and Athukorala and Narayanan (2017).

relationships, and coordinating private participation in all aspects of the ECD, including consultations with the federal government.

Malaysia adopted the good practice of customizing corridors for local advantage, while retaining an overall framework of national development priorities. The corridors are built on existing strengths and resources, as well as on the potential for further economic growth across the corridors. Iskandar Malaysia, for instance, focuses on electrical and electronics industries, petrochemicals, and healthcare, while the Northern Corridor Economic Region focuses on agriculture, logistics, and tourism. The amount of private investment and number of jobs created are two key performance indicators and are monitored by the government. The corridors implicitly compete for public resources to attract private investment, although for different economic emphasis. Aside from implementing projects, anchor investors also participate in consultations with the government on ECD.

Internationally recognized consulting firms were used to undertake feasibility and analysis at the planning stage—an important prerequisite for ECD success. Existing industries are assessed by profitability, growth, and size, as well as a strategic fit for creating jobs, leveraging existing resources, along with future growth and meeting national priorities. For the Northern Corridor Economic Region, for example, more than 30 industries were analyzed before being prioritized for the ECD. The corridor authorities, to some extent, monitored success metrics on how much private investment was mobilized and how many jobs were created in the ECD. This good practice should be undertaken by more ECD planners and should be made more rigorously to ensure targets are met.

Nonetheless, Malaysia's ECDs face challenges in institutional coordination among government bodies at both central and state levels, particularly when their political parties differ. The clearest example is in the Northern Corridor Economic Region, which comprises the states of Penang, Perlis, Perak, and Kedah. Penang is the most economically advanced state as a maritime gateway with highly developed infrastructure and an international airport with much manufacturing integrated into GVCs. However, it is ruled by an opposition party that coordinates poorly with the federal government. The corridor authority is a federal body with the prime minister as chair. Most funding is from the federal government, but it is insufficient to ensure good coordination as the chief minister is from a different party with different priorities. Since 2015, the federal government has prioritized the other participating states, again with poor coordination with Penang. This shows that a strong supranational corridor institution is a good, necessary step but still insufficient to ensure the success of the ECD. Institutional design (e.g., who participates and how funding is structured) also must be considered carefully to ensure effective coordination between diverse government and nongovernment stakeholders.

In sum, all these three corridors are relatively recent and were established within the past 20 years. Except for Malaysia, a middle-income country, most ECDs have been supported by external development partners, and a high-level political commitment is common to all three corridors.[18] Moreover, the broader ECDs in India and Malaysia have support from significant technical and economic analysis with a strong focus on mobilizing private investments. In all cases, ECD management was assigned to a dedicated institution, but the high-level political commitment and institutional management could not avoid problems in coordination, especially across different government levels. These challenges are larger and more likely in ECDs with greater political decentralization and/or more stakeholder participation, particularly those involving multiple countries. On the soft infrastructure of policies and regulations, improving governance and resolving weak project implementation remains a challenge, along with attracting sufficient private investment. These good practices and challenges in ECD are further discussed in Chapter VI.

---

[18]   Leaders of Norther Corridor countries in Eastern Africa, for instance, meet twice a year to review progress.

5 Corridor Programs in ADB's Regional Cooperation and Integration Operations

RCI has been central to ADB's vision and operations from its start in 1966, and ECD has long been recognized as an important part of RCI. ADB's first corporate strategy on RCI—the Regional Cooperation and Integration Strategy in July 2006 (ADB 2006)—highlighted economic corridors' role in boosting connectivity through transport, energy, and trade linkages across regions and subregions. The strategy highlighted the need to adopt a programmatic, comprehensive regional approach to regional corridors and connectivity. It envisioned transport corridors encompassing highways, railways, ports, shipping, and airports.

The strategic view of corridors was further broadened in ADB's Strategy 2030 Operational Plan for Priority 7: Fostering Regional Cooperation and Integration, 2019–2024 (OP7).[19] OP7 cites ECD as a key element in expanding global and regional trade and investment opportunities. It called for ways to develop existing and/or new cross-border economic corridors and to enhance coordination and cooperation among DMCs in trade, finance, or multisector economic corridors. OP7 viewed ECDs as a means to achieve better sector and subsector diversification, from traditional transport and energy sectors to new subsectors—from railways, ports, multimodal transport systems, renewable and clean energy production, and environmental protection to information and ICT, value chains, small and medium-sized enterprises (SMEs), cross-border trade and investment, economic zones, climate change, disaster risk management, and transboundary disease control.

While ambitious, the OP7 view on ECD and its role was not new. Strategically, ADB has long taken an expansive view of economic corridors, evident in the long-term strategies guiding ADB-supported CAREC, GMS, and SASEC subregional cooperation programs. The three subregional cooperation programs are managed mainly by the Regional Cooperation and Integration (RCI) Units of their respective regional departments—Central and West Asia Department (CWRD), Southeast Asia Department (SERD), and South Asia Department (SARD) under ADB's new operating model (NOM). Since Mongolia participates in CAREC and the PRC participates in both CAREC and GMS, the RCI Unit of CWRD is responsible for all CAREC-related issues, including for Mongolia and the PRC, and the RCI Unit of SERD is responsible for all GMS-related issues, including for the PRC, although that Mongolia and PRC are under East Asia Department (EARD). Similarly, the RCI Unit of SARD is responsible for all SASEC-related issues, including Myanmar, although Myanmar is under SERD.[20] The three RCI units work in good coordination and collaboration in supporting the three subregional cooperation programs. This section reviews how far these strategic visions have translated into operations on the ground. In addition to highlighting successes and challenges, lessons are also drawn for further operationalizing ECDs. The review is organized by subregional program, starting with GMS, which has the longest experience with ECD, followed by CAREC and SASEC.

---

19   ADB. 2019. *Strategy 2030 Operational Plan for Priority 7 – Fostering Regional Cooperation and Integration, 2019–2024.* Manila.
20   ADB has placed a temporary hold on sovereign projects and new contracts in Myanmar effective 1 February 2021.

Greater Mekong Subregional Program

Started in 1992, the GMS Program covers Cambodia, the PRC (Yunnan Province and Guangxi Zhuang Autonomous Region), the Lao People's Democratic Republic, Myanmar, Thailand, and Viet Nam. It has supported subregional projects in agriculture, energy, environment, health, and human resource development, ICT, tourism, transport and trade facilitation, and urban development. In 1998, it adopted the ECD approach in developing three cross-border economic corridors—the North-South Economic Corridor (NSEC), the East-West Economic Corridor (EWEC), and the Southern Economic Corridor (SEC). ECD has since remained one of its strategic priorities. A map of the GMS Economic Corridors, along with their sub-corridors is provided in Appendix 1.

Table 1 shows ADB's total lending to GMS during 2009–2020 and for corridor development projects.[21] These are defined by project titles or descriptions that include the terms "corridor," "border economic zone," "sanitary and phytosanitary" (SPS), "transport and trade facilitation" (TTF), "border services," and "border facilities." These terms cover nearly all projects supporting transport, trade, or broader economic corridors with investments in economic zones or towns located along the corridors.

Table 1: Share of Corridor Projects in the GMS Program, 2009–2020

Year Approved	Total GMS Projects ($ million)	Corridor Projects as % of GMS Projects
2009	117.49	100.0
2010	1,009.94	68.4
2011	0	0
2012	381.11	63.9
2013	574.76	100.0
2014	249.12	92.9
2015	338.58	100.0
2016	648.27	80.4
2017	509.40	21.5
2018	1,185.70	88.1
2019	0	0
2020	533.80	90.6
Cumulative	**5,548.17**	**78.5**

GMS = Greater Mekong Subregion.
Source: Asian Development Bank.

There are significant annual variations due to programming and project preparation cycles, but it is nonetheless clear that GMS lending has been corridor-focused. Of the $4.26 billion in loans and grants during 2009–2020 ($5.55 billion including PRC GMS projects), 83.7% (78.5% with PRC projects) allocated for corridor development.

---

[21] Nonlending technical assistance (TA) are not included in the analysis due to difficulty identifying direct links to corridor development. TA projects often cover issues either broader or narrower than the scope of their output. All RCI programs, for example, use so-called umbrella TA projects for secretariat operations that may or may not include funding for specific corridor activities. Many TA projects also last for long periods due to additional financing combined with major or minor changes in scope that may or may not be linked to corridors. For greater clarity, the analysis here is in terms of project volumes rather than numbers, but the conclusions do not change if the number of projects is used.

Table 2 breaks down GMS and corridor projects by sector or area. Transport, urban development (water and other urban infrastructure and services), and industry and trade account for more than 90% of lending, with transport alone accounting for 59.4%. It should be noted that the volume of lending for "software" such as TTF and SPS—cross-border corridor sections—is typically small but generally high in importance and impact.

Table 2: Sector Shares in GMS and GMS Corridor Projects, Cumulative 2009–2020
(%)

Sector/Activity of GMS and Corridor Projects	GMS	Corridor
Agriculture, natural resources, and rural development	7.6	5.1
Education	4.5	0
Energy	0.4	0
Health	4.3	0
Industry and trade	8.8	10.9
Sanitary and phytosanitary	0.6	0.8
Transport	55.0	59.4
Transport and trade facilitation	0.2	0.2
Water and other urban infrastructure and services	18.5	23.6
Total	**100.0**	**100.0**

GMS = Greater Mekong Subregion.
Source: Asian Development Bank.

The dominance of the transport sector in corridor projects underlines that the GMS Program has a narrow, linear focus on ECD in the form of transport (and transit) corridors. This may reflect the initial conditions in the GMS countries during the program's early years, where basic regional transport connectivity was underdeveloped, particularly for those member countries previously in conflict with one another.

Table 2 also shows that during 2009–2020 the GMS Program began widening the scope of corridor operations, with two non-transport sectors accounting for almost one-third of all corridor lending. This is further highlighted by the growing importance of urban development, industry and trade starting in 2012 (Table 3).

Despite the early adoption of ECD, GMS investments initially focused on linear M-type corridors. It is encouraging that, over the past decade, the GMS Program has increasingly broadened its ECD approach.

The shift in GMS operations around 2012 was consistent with the then new GMS Strategic Framework (2012–2022) that also marked a clear strategic move toward a more spatial approach to ECD. The GMS Ha Noi Action Plan (2018–2022), still in effect, continues to amplify this shift given its core spatial orientation—expanding the concept of the economic corridor beyond just a transport and transit route. This expanded approach to developing economic corridors would include (i) urban development to widen the corridor space for connecting markets and exploiting agglomeration effects, (ii) development of SEZs and industrial parks at the borders and along corridors as vehicles for private investment, and (iii) development of transport and logistics services to enhance links with trade gateways and to make markets function more efficiently. These are the "second generation" investments envisaged under the strategic framework.

Table 3: Sector Shares in GMS Corridor Projects, 2009–2020
(%)

Year Approved	Agriculture, natural resources, and rural development	Industry and trade	SPS	Transport	TTF	Water and other urban infrastructure and services
2009	0	0	0	100.0	0	0
2010	10.1	0	0	68.1	0	21.7
2011	0	0	0	0	0	0
2012	0	0	14.7	0	0	85.3
2013	10.5	0	0	89.5	0	0
2014	0	37.2	0	62.8	0	0
2015	0	0	0	50.5	0	49.5
2016	0	24.9	0	75.1	0	0
2017	0	0	0	90.9	9.1	0
2018	8.6	24.6	0	18.6	0	48.1
2019	0	0	0	0	0	0
2020	0	0	0	100.0	0.0	0.0
2009–2020	**5.1**	**10.9**	**0.8**	**59.4**	**0.2**	**23.6**

GMS = Greater Mekong Subregion, SPS = sanitary and phytosanitary, TTF = transport and trade facilitation.
Source: Asian Development Bank.

The latest long-term GMS Strategic Framework (GMS-2030), endorsed in 2021, continues building on these trends by repeatedly emphasizing the use of a spatial approach in operations: *"GMS-2030 will deepen the spatial approach to development by expanding the network of economic corridors throughout the subregion, building upon existing transport corridors to maximize network effects and connections between corridors to promote growth and transform key corridor sections into full-fledged economic corridors"* (GMS-2030, p. 50). The framework recognizes the program's earlier operational emphasis on M-type corridors while underscoring the need to apply an S-type approach in "key corridor sections."

Central Asia Regional Economic Cooperation Program

Established in 2001, CAREC includes 11 member countries—Afghanistan, Azerbaijan, PRC (Xinjiang Uygur Autonomous Region and Inner Mongolia Autonomous Region), Georgia, Kazakhstan, Kyrgyz Republic, Mongolia, Pakistan, Tajikistan, Turkmenistan, and Uzbekistan.[22] In its early years of operations, it focused on three traditional sectors—transport, energy, and trade (trade policy and trade facilitation). ADB invited other development partners to co-lead the program, such as the World Bank (energy), the International Monetary Fund (trade policy), and the United Nations Development Programme ("soft" issues and human development). ADB led transport and trade facilitation, and by helping create CAREC's Joint Transport and Trade Facilitation Strategy 2006, it mapped out six transport corridors anticipating them to become ECDs over time.

---

[22] ADB placed on hold its regular assistance to Afghanistan effective 15 August 2021. https://www.adb.org/news/adb-statement-afghanistan.

Following the approval of the CAREC 2030 strategy in 2017, the program expanded to five operational clusters: (i) economic and financial stability; (ii) trade, tourism, and economic corridors; (iii) infrastructure and economic connectivity; (iv) agriculture and water; and (v) human development. Integrating ICT across CAREC operations was a crosscutting priority.

CAREC 2030 retains a strong link between ECD and external trade, emphasizing its importance for agglomeration and urbanization in boosting trade flows. As CAREC 2030 notes, *"Economic corridors exploit the strong growth effects of agglomeration that accompanies urbanization; these effects are amplified if resilient infrastructure linkages exist, and conditions are propitious for private sector investments. The integrated space within economic corridors relies upon free movements of labor and capital and trade and investment flows. Successful corridors require economic density, as well as corridor-wide energy and transport linkages"* (p. 11). CAREC has made a point of moving into the more complex S-type approach.

CAREC's latest strategic approach to ECD is far from its past operational approach, which focused on basic M-type transport corridors with some elements of transit (border management infrastructure) corridor development (Tables 4, 5, and 6).

Table 4: Corridor Projects in the CAREC Program, 2010–2020

Year Approved	Total CAREC Projects ($ million)	Corridor Share of CAREC Projects (%)
2010	1,165.8	50.9
2011	1,452.6	61.7
2012	1,595.4	57.3
2013	892.7	21.1
2014	939.6	57.1
2015	794.1	52.4
2016	863.1	51.0
2017	1,112.0	59.4
2018	997.8	16.8
2019	1,306.8	74.9
2020	616.2	49.4
Cumulative	**11,736.2**	**51.9**

CAREC = Central Asia Regional Economic Cooperation.
Source: Asian Development Bank.

Table 5: Sector Share in CAREC and CAREC Corridor Projects, Cumulative 2010–2020
(%)

Sector/Activity	CAREC	Corridor
Energy	21.0	0
Industry and trade	2.0	0.5
RIBS	2.7	5.3
SPS	0.1	0.2
Transport	74.2	94.0
Total	**100.0**	**100.0**

CAREC = Central Asia Regional Economic Cooperation.
Source: Asian Development Bank.

Table 6: Sector Share in CAREC Corridor Projects, 2010–2020
(%)

Year Approved	Industry and Trade	RIBS	SPS	Transport
2010	0	0	0	100.0
2011	0	0	0	100.0
2012	0	0	0	100.0
2013	0	9.3	0	90.7
2014	0	0	0	100.0
2015	0	59.7	3.5	36.8
2016	0	6.2	0	93.8
2017	0	0	0	100.0
2018	0	0	0	100.0
2019	0	2.8	0	97.2
2020	10.0	0	0	90.0
2010–2020	**0.5**	**5.3**	**0.2**	**94.0**

CAREC = Central Asia Regional Economic Cooperation, RIBS = Regional Improvement of Border Services, SPS = sanitary and phytosanitary.
Source: Asian Development Bank.

CAREC's focus on transport and transit corridors is appropriate given the economic geography of the subregion—characterized by low population density, vast distances, landlocked members, and geographical features such as mountainous terrain and deserts. Given the improved regional transport corridors over the past 2 decades, CAREC's new focus on S-type, agglomeration-driven ECD responds to current needs. For example, the pilot Almaty–Bishkek Economic Corridor (ABEC) builds on existing transport infrastructure between urban clusters to focus on the ECD agglomeration approach. ABEC has made good progress on the background analytical work necessary to build consensus among participants, identify a pipeline of interventions, and establish supranational institutional mechanisms.

ABEC initiatives are part of an agenda of bilateral intergovernmental meetings chaired by the respective members' prime ministers. Physical investment projects in agriculture, transport, health, tourism, and other areas are being developed and/or financed.[23]

Initiated in 2018, the most recent CAREC corridor is the STKEC, focused on three geographically adjacent cities in Kazakhstan, Uzbekistan, and Tajikistan, respectively, and their surrounding provinces (regions). The six priority thematic areas of the STKEC road map include the traditional transport and transit elements but also have a strong regional development focus emphasizing agricultural value chains, regional tourism, SEZs and industrial zones.[24] Appendix 2 provides maps of two CAREC economic corridors.

South Asia Subregional Economic Cooperation Program

Launched in 2001, SASEC comprises Bangladesh, Bhutan, India, Maldives, Myanmar, Nepal, and Sri Lanka. It initially focused on six areas—transport; energy; tourism; ICT; the environment; and trade, investment, and private sector cooperation. In 2011, the program began concentrating on three sectors—transport, trade facilitation, and energy (ADB 2016b). Tables 7, 8, and 9 show the total volume of SASEC lending during 2009–2020, the share of projects identified as corridor projects (less than other programs at 44%), and the cumulative sector shares for the same period. Transport accounts for 74.1% of the projects and energy for 13.2%, with the rest comprising trade facilitation. SASEC projects are responsive to the needs of the region, which are improved transport connectivity and energy trade, which has significant potential.

Table 7: Share of Corridor Projects in SASEC, 2009–2020

Year Approved	Total SASEC Projects ($ million)	Corridor Share of SASEC Projects (%)
2009	183.0	0
2010	177.1	0
2011	448.5	0
2012	256.1	93.5
2013	273.8	0
2014	1,055.6	92.4
2015	149.6	0
2016	1,424.5	27.4
2017	474.1	100.0
2018	650.0	0
2019	1,303.9	76.2
2020	602.2	0.7
Cumulative	**6,998.5**	**44.0**

SASEC = South Asia Subregional Economic Cooperation.
Source: Asian Development Bank.

---

[23] ADB. 2014. *Operationalizing Economic Corridors in Central Asia: A case study of the Almaty–Bishkek Corridor*. Manila, and Rosbach, Kristian. 2019. *Testing the 3D approach to economic corridor development in Central Asia*. Asian Development Blog. 6 February. https://blogs.adb.org/blog/testing-3d-approach-economic-corridor-development-central-asia.
[24] ADB. 2021. *A Roadmap for Shymkent-Tashkent-Khujand Economic Corridor*. Manila.

Table 8: Sector Share in SASEC and SASEC Corridor Projects, Cumulative 2012–2020
(%)

Sector/Activity	SASEC	Corridor
Energy	22.3	13.8
Industry and trade	0.1	4.1
Transport	73.8	74.1
Transport and trade facilitation	1.3	2.9
Water and other urban infrastructure and services	2.5	5.1
Total	**100.0**	**100.0**

SASEC = South Asia Subregional Economic Cooperation.
Source: Asian Development Bank.

Table 9: Sector Share of SASEC Corridor Projects, 2012–2020
(%)

Year Approved	Energy	Industry and Trade	Transport	TTF	Water and Other Urban Infrastructure and Services
2012	0	0	80.2	19.8	0
2013	0	0	0	0	0
2014	18.4	0	81.6	0	0
2015	0	0	0	0	0
2016	62.9	32.1	0	5.0	0
2017	0	0	63.3	4.6	32.1
2018	0	0	0	0	0
2019	0	0	100.0	0	0
2020	0	0	0	0	100
2012–2020	**13.8**	**4.1**	**74.1**	**2.9**	**5.1**

SASEC = South Asia Subregional Economic Cooperation, TTF = transport and trade facilitation.
Source: Asian Development Bank.

The year 2016 was a turning point in SASEC's operations as the program adopted its first comprehensive long-term plan (ADB 2016b)—the SASEC Operational Plan 2016–2025, which also added ECD as a fourth pillar, complementing transport, trade facilitation, and energy. The SASEC Operational Plan's approach to ECD is regional development: *"The development of economic corridors depends on transport infrastructure as the backbone that will enable economic activities. By expanding development beyond the narrow space of a transport route and developing areas between them, the benefits are spread further to the hinterlands, thus contributing to inclusive growth"* (p. 19). The regional development orientation to ECD is further underlined by the strategic approach in the SASEC Operational Plan *"The key factors to consider in formulating specific plans for ECD are (i) identifying the locus of economic potentials within a transport corridor and the potential backward and forward linkages for industries, including across regional and global supply chains; (ii) reducing trade costs and barriers;*

(iii) developing the network of feeder and rural roads; and (iv) determining the role of urban centers. ECD would need to consider important links across sectors and the critical initiatives that would enable markets to develop." (p. 20). Appendix 3 provides a map of SASEC economic corridors.

An example of SASEC's explicit S-type ECD approach is the Vizag-Chennai Industrial Corridor, supported by ADB, which runs across southern India's eastern coast (ADB 2016). Three other SASEC ECD projects during 2017–2020 follow the Vizag-Chennai corridor, including two urban development projects and one transport project. These marked the second phase of ADB support to the East Coast Economic Corridor, of which the Vizag-Chennai Industrial Corridor is a part.[25] Another two S-type ECD projects approved in 2021 were in industry and trade, and urban development.

Discussion

ADB's long experience with economic corridors provides a wealth of insights and valuable lessons for operationalizing the development of economic corridors in Asia and the Pacific in the future. Early work on the GMS Program provided a model for the ensuing CAREC and SASEC subregional programs. The GMS vision from its start (in 1992) was couched in building transport networks to facilitate regional development. This S-type regional-development approach was evident by calling all major transport corridors "economic corridors"—the NSEC, EWEC, and the SEC. For GMS, as well as for CAREC and SASEC, ECD and RCI were strongly linked by their focus on promoting trade.

Unlike its broader vision, the operational focus of GMS was on M-type transport corridors, which is clear from the project data (see Tables 1, 2, and 3). Soon, the program introduced transit and trade interventions with a push for the GMS Cross-Border Trade Agreement (CBTA). This marked a shift toward building a trade corridor, but still an M-type ECD.

The M-type approach to ECD focused on basic transport corridors, carried over into both CAREC and SASEC programs. The data show the CAREC program had the highest transport intensity even during 2009–2020. The transport-dominated M-type corridor approach shows how well the subregional programs responded to the subregion's history and geography. All ADB-supported subregional programs soon moved toward a trade (transport and transit) corridor approach. While GMS focused on its CBTA, which is dominated by transport, CAREC focused on improving border infrastructure and procedures while SASEC focused on trade-facilitation needs of landlocked Nepal.[26]

In general, ADB-supported subregional programs have had considerable success with transport corridors. This is less so with the shift into trade corridors. Transforming GMS transport corridors into trade corridors has shown limited progress. CAREC's success with transit and border management initiatives has similarly shown less progress than in developing basic transport corridors. The ABEC and STKEC remain in the early stages of development. SASEC, however, adopted an integrated S-type regional development approach to ECD that was attached to the ambitious government program to develop major industrial corridors. The SASEC Operational Plan's ECD strategy is to *"promoting synergies between economic corridors being developed in individual SASEC countries and optimizing*

---

[25] The second phase extends from Chennai to Kanyakumari, where ADB has already committed more than $1.4 billion in transport, energy, urban, and industrial infrastructure development.

[26] SASEC's responsiveness to regional needs and economic geography makes its transport corridor a little different from the other two programs. SASEC focused on improving transport networks within its larger members rather than across them. Geographically, an overwhelmingly larger proportion of manufacturing in its largest member, India, is concentrated in the south and southwest, while most other members are northeast or east of the country, except Maldives, which is an archipelago well south of India's southwestern coastline.

development impacts of economic corridor investments through improved cross-border links." This approach also highlights the critical importance of strong government ownership and partnership for ECD.

Over 2010–2020, all three ADB-supported subregional programs have shifted their strategies toward the S-type or "spatial" approach to ECD. Starting with the GMS in 2012, more corridor investments were made in non-transport areas: for example, urban development in towns along transport corridors, agriculture (including SPS), tourism, and cross-border economic zones. The ABEC is an innovative agglomeration-driven ECD with a relatively smaller share of transport projects. The newest CAREC economic corridor, the STKEC, has both transport and trade components but also incorporates significant regional development. SASEC introduced its first coastal economic corridor, the Vizag-Chennai Industrial Corridor, as part of the East Coast Economic Corridor that rests on a transport spine but holds a large portfolio of road networks surrounding it, along with urban development, industrial zones, and industrial development. It also includes institutional and governance elements in its ECD package. This integrated approach contrasts with earlier GMS corridor development, which used more isolated interventions but has now shifted directly to an increasingly spatial approach.[27]

To conclude, ADB's RCI operations converged during its first 2 decades into a consistent framework for M-type corridors. This M-type corridor approach was most successful in the early stage of ECD (transport corridors) in response to the region's needs but with mixed results in transforming transport corridors into trade corridors. Over 2010–2020, ADB's RCI operations started moving toward the broader S-type ECD that seeks to go beyond the early success of M-type corridors. The actual implementation of the spatial approach of ECD has not been easy, with progress varied and little coordination across subregions. Thus, a new ECD framework that operationalizes the S-type economic corridors will help facilitate the emerging transition to the next generation ECD initiatives.

---

[27]   GMS 2030 cites insufficient integration across sectors and themes as a program weakness (p. 12).

6 Framework for Economic Corridor Development

This chapter develops a framework for ECD based on the ideas and concepts in chapters 2 and 3 and the corridor experience in chapters 4 and 5. It starts with three ECD tenets: (i) economic corridors are intrinsically spatial; (ii) they are defined by an identified spatial area and a set of economic activities and markets in that area; and (iii) ECD is the process of widening and deepening the set of economic activities in the area by providing necessary infrastructure, developing and linking markets in the area, and creating or strengthening the institutions that support the expected increase in the density of economic activities. ECD is thus multisector and multi-vector, requiring a potentially wide array of interventions. ECD may comprise some or all of the diverse infrastructure investments required—such as transport networks, power grids, ICT, urban development, and human capital through health and education—along with the policies that promote economic sectors (agriculture, industry, and services), the regulatory reforms needed to make markets work better, and institutional innovations.

Conceptual Framework

Generally, ECD consists of several potential interventions, such as hard infrastructure investments, along with policy and institutional reforms. Together, these interventions aim to increase the economic mass and density of the targeted space in terms of the types of economic activities being undertaken, along with their form, scale, and scope. To illustrate, a simple ECD may be a transport corridor connecting two urban centers, with an immediate or intermediate effect of saving time and vehicle operating costs for those using the corridor. The final impact may include an integrated labor market between the two centers, greater access for rural producers tapping urban markets, improved women's welfare due to increased economic opportunities, and environmental degradation (e.g., pollution caused by increased traffic). A broader ECD may be a transport corridor linking two urban centers in different countries combined with the policy reforms needed for TTF. An even broader ECD may consist of a cross-border transport corridor, other transport networks, TTF, border economic zones, and public health interventions to prevent or mitigate cross-border transmission of infectious diseases. Many combinations are possible as they are seen in practice across different economies and subregions.

In principle, an ECD is a combination of many hardware or physical infrastructure investments, software or policies, and regulations linked to the optimal use of the hardware, along with the soft components that improve markets, governance, the business and investment climate, and the other elements essential for a successful economic corridor. Not all interventions are relevant to all situations, and each intervention package will have its own costs. The decision for an ECD planner is to determine what is the optimal ECD—the best combination of possible interventions that maximize the benefits of the program net of intervention costs.

Figure 2 illustrates the factors that affect the benefits of ECD interventions and their costs.[28] Starting from the top left of the figure, the benefits of any ECD depend upon structural factors characterizing the corridor area—such as availability of a skilled workforce, firm density, business environment, or regional connectivity. The initial conditions for these structural factors at the start of the ECD will, in turn, be affected by geographic and economic constraints—first and second nature forces—that affect the area. For example, a biotech sector development-focused ECD will yield benefits that are affected by the availability of skilled labor and quality research institutions. Similarly, interventions that improve trade facilitation produce benefits depending on whether the area can access seaports and the quality of its business environment.

Figure 2: Economic Corridor Development Conceptual Framework

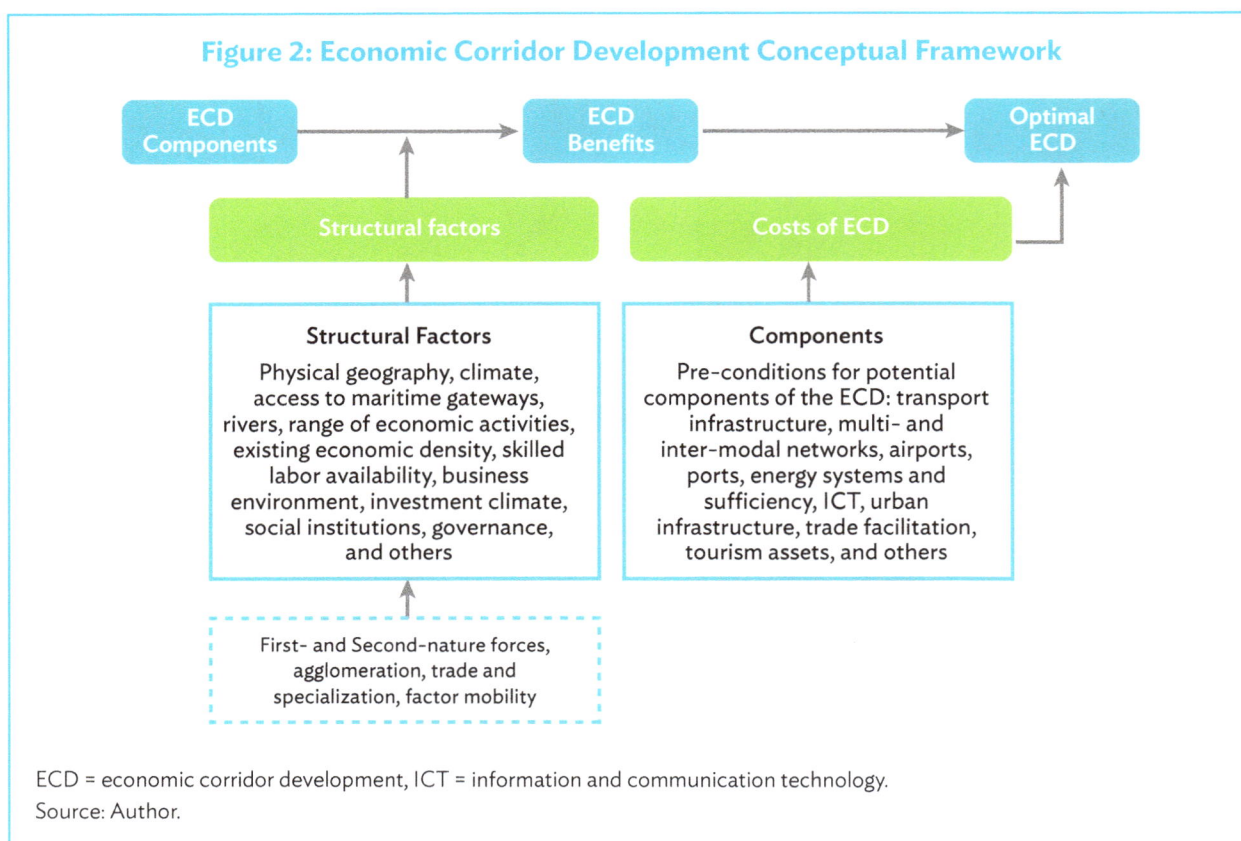

ECD = economic corridor development, ICT = information and communication technology.
Source: Author.

Conversely, the costs of any specific ECD intervention will be proportional to its own initial condition. For example, the costs of urban infrastructure development will be proportional to the existing levels of infrastructure, while the costs of improving last-mile connectivity will depend on existing road networks. The two types of initial conditions defining the corridor space—potential ECD intervention and structural attributes of the area—define what an optimal ECD will look like (Box 2).

---

[28]   Box 2 more formally identifies what makes an ECD optimal.

Box 2: Identifying the Optimal Economic Corridor Development

Let the set of various intervention components of an economic corridor development (ECD) be denoted by the vector E. Depending on the type of ECD, the vector E may characterize physical investments, policy reforms, institutional initiatives, and any other components that may lead to the desired development of the economic corridor. The cost of the ECD will depend upon the pre-existing conditions characterizing the spatial region. For example, the cost of a transport investment may be less if it is only upgrading existing roads than if it is building new ones. As another example, the cost of trade and transport facilitation (TTF) interventions may be less if the existing trade infrastructure at border crossings is already of sufficient quality or if the required software is already in place with people trained to use it. Let the vector $\bar{E}$ denote the pre-existing values of the corresponding components of ECD vector and the costs of the ECD as $(E-\bar{E})^2$.

Similarly, let the vector denote the final economic benefits (for example, economic welfare, gross domestic product (GDP) growth, job creation, human capital indices, equity, inclusivity, and climate resilience, among others) from the ECD interventions. Then the optimal ECD denoted E is the solution to the problem:

$$\max_{E} \quad B'B - (E-\bar{E})^2 \tag{1}$$

Where, as noted, B is the vector comprising the ultimate benefits of the ECD. Equation 1 denotes that while designing an optimal ECD, the policy maker would seek to maximize these benefits net of costs.

The optimization is subject to two constraints. The first describes how the ECD package affects the targeted benefits B conditional on other structural factors (X). Or,

$$B = f(E, X) \tag{2}$$

where f is a general function describing the relationship between benefits and ECD interventions. The structural factors X represent local conditions that may strengthen or weaken the effects of E on B. For example, when considering a transport corridor, its growth benefits may be affected by soil or climate conditions in the area, the density of firms already existing in the space, or whether there is a gateway port at one end of the proposed corridor, or whether the space is characterized by well-developed financial services that can mobilize savings into investments.

The second constraint to the ECD optimization in equation (1) denotes the fact that the structural factors X can themselves change during ECD implementation. For example, a transport corridor may lead to greater firm density in the affected space as firms or skilled labor relocate due to reduced transport costs and better business prospects. Again, the extent to which X will change in response to interventions E will be dependent on the status of X before the interventions occur—pre-existing situation for X, denoted by $\bar{X}$, (which in turn will be influenced by the First and Second nature forces affecting the area). For example, an area with a pleasant climate, all else equal, will be more attractive for firms and labor to locate even before any ECD implementation. This is described in equation (3) using g to denote the functional form of the relationship.

$$X = g(E, \bar{X}) \tag{3}$$

Solving the optimization problem and its constraints (equations (1)-(3)) gives the optimal ECD E^* as a function of the pre-existing or initial conditions (the structural factors and elements of the ECD).

$$E^* = h(\bar{E}, \bar{X}) \tag{4}$$

In principle, by solving equation (4) a planner can determine which particular package of interventions would yield the best possible results for the targeted ECD. The best or optimal ECD will depend upon many factors that characterize the starting point (of proposed interventions) and structural attributes of the area.

Source: Authors' elaboration of Roberts, Mark, Martin Melecky Théophile Bougna Yan (Sarah) Xu. 2018. Transport corridors and their wider economic benefits: A critical review of the literature. *Policy Research Working Paper*. No. 8302. Washington, DC: World Bank.

Taking into consideration its general nature, this conceptual framework underlines seven important insights for planning, developing and implementing ECDs.

First, it is important to recognize the wide spectrum of relevant factors when designing an ECD. The ultimate benefits or effectiveness of an ECD depends on a host of structural factors and initial (pre-ECD) conditions characterizing the proposed interventions. Even an intervention like a simple transport corridor is ill-served by focusing only on saving travel time and vehicle operating costs. Its design and ultimate impact will improve if attention is paid to some of the initial structural conditions characterizing the targeted area, such as physical geography, land and labor markets, and even social norms, such as women's participation in economic activities. When considering these factors, attention should be paid to the transmission mechanism between the immediate outcomes of interventions (such as reduced travel time) and subsequent transmission mechanisms from the intermediate outcomes to the final desired outcomes (like job creation).

Second, the suitability of any area considered for an ECD depends on several initial conditions and structural factors that characterize the area—preconditions for an ECD.[29] Areas with extremely low levels of economic activity due to geographical constraints (first nature forces) or poor economic levels (second nature forces) may not be suitable for an ECD. The costs of any proposed interventions in isolated mountain settings, for example, or isolated rural communities, will likely outweigh any possible benefits. ECD cannot create economic density in a vacuum. Just like a transport corridor "from nowhere to nowhere through nowhere" cannot create significant benefits, an ECD must target spatial domains that have some underlying potential. At the other end of the spectrum, geographical areas that are already highly developed with high-density of economic activities may not benefit from ECD interventions due to a lack of identifiable interventions that offer significant benefits (though they may anchor or contribute to ECDs in areas linked to them).

Third, the benefits of ECD may be diminished unless the target group of beneficiaries is large enough, indicating an ECD may face challenges in sparsely populated areas. For any given set of ECD components, the benefits will be proportional to the number of potential beneficiaries. With too few beneficiaries, the costs of any conceivable ECD may exceed its benefits (negative net benefits).

Fourth, an ECD with even modest scope—a few interventions coupled with complementary policies and institutional interventions—can expand into considerable complexity. For example, ADB's experience with ECDs has shown difficulties in implementing "software" projects. This also characterized the other type of corridors discussed in chapter III, which identified the challenges of institutional development for ECD. A combination of physical investments with policies for software and institutions can have complex chains of interactions and consequences. An obvious implication is the critical need for extensive analytical and empirical analysis as foundational inputs into the ECD design.

While complex and challenging, there are practical examples of this ECD approach. Two examples within the region were discussed in chapters III and IV—the preparatory approach to the Northern Corridor in Malaysia and the East Coast Economic Corridor under SASEC. In both cases, comprehensive technical and economic analysis preceded and became part of the ECD design and planning.

---

[29]   Sugiyarto and Mushtaq (2021) propose a similar framework with these preconditions at its core, upon which then ECD uses the three pillars of infrastructure, urban development, and industrial development, complemented by three crosscutting drivers—software (institutions and regulations), economic and technical analysis, and sustainability and inclusiveness.

Fifth, every ECD is unique. The targeted objectives of the ECD, the proposed menu of interventions, the initial preconditions for the proposed interventions, and the structural preconditions of the space targeted for ECD, taken together, offer virtually infinite combinations. The details of any economic corridor and its development will all vary from situation to situation. Each economic corridor is thus unique.

Sixth, there is no single formula for ECD. What can be common across different corridors is the methodology used for designing an ECD in the form of principles and good practices. These could guide customized, careful consideration of ECD objectives for the targeted area and the interventions that would best achieve the objectives given the corridor's initial conditions and structural attributes. Other considerations, such as political context, resource constraints, and the time horizon, for example, would naturally affect the core methodology.

Finally, as the size and scope of an ECD expand, the increased complexity of design also implies the need for greater funding and requirements for "soft infrastructure." This requires more partnerships with the private sector and development partners, increasing the number of stakeholders and required coordination.

Operational Framework

Based on the conceptual framework described above, this operational framework for ECD was developed to guide the practical implementation of ECD by partitioning decision-making into smaller and distinct zones. These zones can serve three important purposes: (i) clarify the objectives of an ECD, (ii) identify the initial conditions for designing an ECD, and (iii) define a sequence or phasing for ECD implementation.

The four zones use the M-type and S-type categories described in chapter II, supplemented by considering whether the decision space is domestic or cross-border (Figure 3).[30] The vertical axis represents the transition from an M-type to S-type framework. The geographical scope of the ECD is depicted on the horizontal axis, ranging from a domestic or national economic corridor to a regional or cross-border economic corridor. This allows the partitioning of a potential ECD into four zones. Each zone can potentially reflect the ECD goal for operational purposes. There is no automatic "transformation" from one zone to another. Taken together, the four zones outline the implementation phases of an ECD. Finally, the zones can also become a reference for baselining the initial conditions for an ECD. An ECD can be launched from any set of initial conditions—which determine the right program for an ECD.

Zone I, at its most basic, represents a domestic transport corridor—a prerequisite to any ECD—in which the priority is to improve connectivity and reduce transport costs within the target area. In practice, this may mean new infrastructure or rehabilitating existing infrastructure, building a transport network rather than a single artery. Given the relative importance of hardware investments, Zone I requires considerable financial resources for any high-impact infrastructure development or improvements. Experience has shown this is relatively less complex to manage. Increased complexity characterizes any transition from Zone I to either Zone II or Zone III.

---

[30] The analysis here draws upon Srivastava (2013) and FAO (2017).

Figure 3: Four Zones for Operationalizing Economic Corridor Development

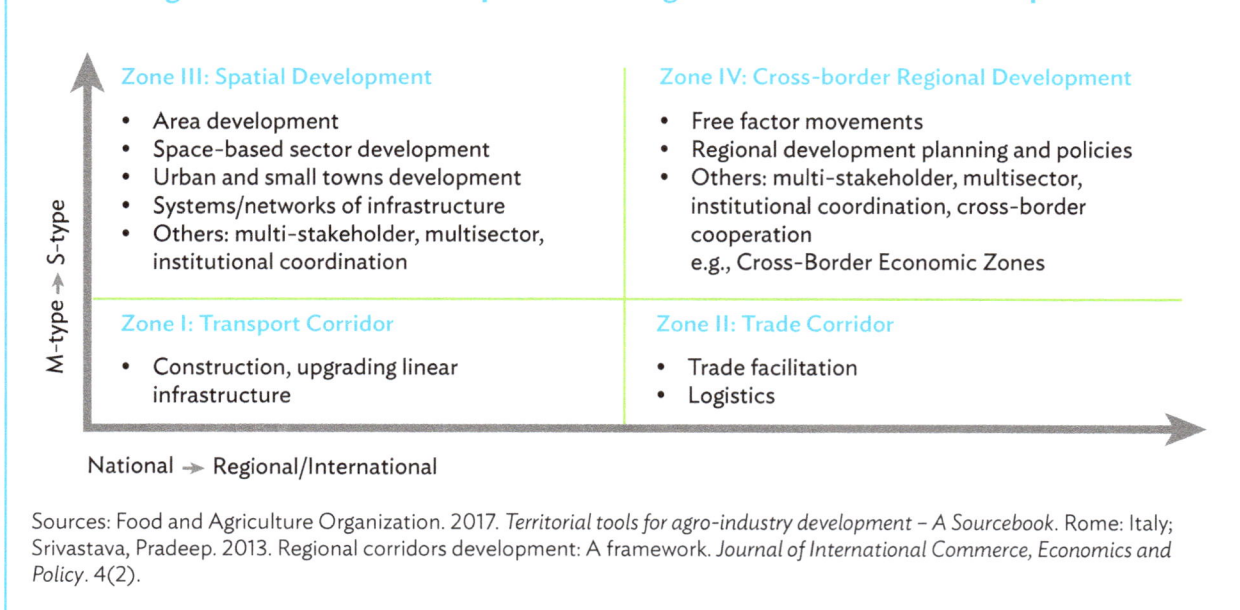

Zone III: Spatial Development

- Area development
- Space-based sector development
- Urban and small towns development
- Systems/networks of infrastructure
- Others: multi-stakeholder, multisector, institutional coordination

Zone IV: Cross-border Regional Development

- Free factor movements
- Regional development planning and policies
- Others: multi-stakeholder, multisector, institutional coordination, cross-border cooperation
  e.g., Cross-Border Economic Zones

Zone I: Transport Corridor

- Construction, upgrading linear infrastructure

Zone II: Trade Corridor

- Trade facilitation
- Logistics

M-type → S-type

National → Regional/International

Sources: Food and Agriculture Organization. 2017. *Territorial tools for agro-industry development – A Sourcebook*. Rome: Italy; Srivastava, Pradeep. 2013. Regional corridors development: A framework. *Journal of International Commerce, Economics and Policy*. 4(2).

Zone II retains the focus on movement but adds the complexity of managing cross-border trade. It signifies an intention to integrate the national corridor into a regional framework, to promote regional cooperation by working on trade facilitation and logistics, and to improve regional coordination and planning. As a stand-alone objective, Zone II requires improving regional physical connectivity (hardware) but also incorporates (software) interventions such as enhancing border policies and TTF as primary components. Experience (as in chapters 3 and 4) has shown this is more challenging than a Zone I ECD, but Zone II uses a relatively standard methodology—intervention points—even if complete success has been difficult to achieve in most practical cases.

For the purposes of this guidance note, ECD is meaningful only if its objectives are within Zone III and Zone IV, which both mark a significant jump in complexity from Zone I or Zone II. An ECD designed for Zone III expands (Zone I) corridor interventions to a wider spectrum that could include value chain development, area development plans, development of agricultural and/or industrial clusters, SEZs, industrial targeting, urban development, and services—such as finance, business development, and tourism—necessary to exploit territorial advantages and stimulate economic growth.[31] Infrastructure development remains fundamental, but its scope is far greater than a transport corridor. It includes multimodal transport networks, energy grids, irrigation, ICT, water and sanitation, and last-mile infrastructure such as rural roads that can integrate a broader area into the local economy.

Zone IV represents the most ambitious ECD, adding cross-border coordination and cooperation across the multiple dimensions of Zones II and III interventions, such as trade facilitation, cross-border logistics, transport facilitation, labor standards, factor mobility, private-investment promotion, cross-border institutional mechanisms for corridor development, as well as cooperation on RPGs, among others.

---

[31]   This is also consistent with the framework proposed by Sugiyarto and Mushtaq op. cit.

Starting from Zone I, corridor development can move into either Zone II or Zone III, or both. However, a direct shift into Zone IV may not be practical. In this sense, Zone I may be considered an interim stage for either Zone II or Zone III, with all three zones considered a prerequisite to moving into Zone IV.

When the zones are viewed as stages in ECD implementation, it is worth noting that the transition from one zone to another is not a discrete event but a process, with each zone holding various levels of intensity or development. For example, even the basic Zone I can have various degrees of transport connectivity, from single to multiple divided lanes to the quality of the transport corridor in terms of road signage, road safety, and roadside facilities, among others. Differing degrees can apply to deepening transport networks in the target ECD area. An ECD can also be based on an explicit masterplan targeting any of the zones, with interim zones (if any) representing implementation phases. In other situations, ECD planners may be asked to start from an interim zone with the objective of formulating a strategy that targets a more complex zone. The interim zone then defines the initial conditions within the ECD masterplan with potential pathways to the new ECD objective.

Most ECDs under ADB-supported subregional programs started in Zone I without an explicit plan for an S-type ECD. Over time they made progress toward Zone II with mixed success. Over the past decade, the GMS Program aimed to shift toward Zone III but relied only on opportunistic interventions not integrated into explicit masterplan or bespoke corridor institutions. Most recent SASEC initiatives have designed ECDs explicitly for Zone II, with Zone I as an interim implementation phase, with some space for Zone III projects included in the initial plans. Similarly, most CAREC corridors, like those in GMS, have focused primarily on Zone I with mixed attempts to move into Zone II. The most recent CAREC ECDs have targeted Zone IV, or a combination of Zones II and III (though STKEC is still under development).

For RCI operations, it is also important that there is no presumption of normative ranking across the four ECD zones. ADB may support its DMCs in all four categories. Under the current framework, each corridor is unique, responding to the defined objectives of DMCs, customized to local initial conditions and structural factors that also shape the desirability of ECD components. There are many parts of Asia and the Pacific where Zone I may be the best development tool under existing conditions and objectives, and many other parts where Zone II may yield good results if successful. For example, several parts of Central Asia and the Caucasus may be best placed for Zone II or Zone I programs over the short to medium term, while Zone III or Zone IV may be suitable for some countries. Greater ECD complexity does not mean there is a higher development impact under all conditions.

From this perspective, the specific ECD targeted (whether for Zone I or Zone IV) is not a critical issue. What matters is to identify the suitable zone, specify the starting point and/or zone, and map the pathway to the target zone at the start of the ECD. There is enough experience over the past 2 decades to confirm that piecemeal approaches (in Zone I, for example) and hopeful invocations are simply not enough to "transform" into a higher and more complex zone of ECD.

The next section further grounds the framework for operational teams and planners by providing guiding principles and good practices for ECD, drawing upon the framework described and the lessons learned from the review of corridors in practice (chapters IV and V). The guiding principles are not prescriptive, as each economic corridor is unique, and each country and region have its own history, topography, culture, and political context (or First and Second nature forces). Whenever considering an ECD, countries, and planners will need to make sound choices even as they face complex trade-offs and challenges.

Guiding Principles

The operational stages in designing an ECD can be quite similar for all four ECD zones. Even a basic transport corridor in Zone I will require an initial conceptualization or "proof-of-concept" stage, followed by a more detailed feasibility study, engineering design, resource mobilization, implementation, and finally, a monitoring and evaluation phase. While these phases may be similar to more complex ECDs, the details of each phase will be spread on a much broader canvas. The discussion that follows is in the context of formulating a Zone IV ECD.[32]

Stage 1: Corridor conceptualization and/or proof-of-concept. For an ECD, the first step is an overall vision for the economic corridor. This "visioning" exercise must answer several critical questions:

- What form will the corridor take when completed?
- What problems will it solve, or what objectives will it help achieve?
- What is its technical justification? Is it the best approach, or are there other ways to address the same problems (for example, relying on other instruments, such as industrial parks or SEZs, or relying on market forces and private capital)?
- What geographic area (which may include one or more FEAs) will define the ECD? Choosing the appropriate geographic area is important to an ECD as an economic corridor can amplify and synergize economic forces but not create something out of nothing. The existing economic potential of the identified areas, and potential natural advantages or constraints, should be carefully considered.
- What are the other initial conditions for the proposed ECD? For a Zone IV corridor, what stage is the identified geographic area in terms of a Zone II and/or Zone III ECD?
- What initial sectoral growth drivers are envisaged for the ECD, depending on the existing initial conditions of the corridor region?
- Will the envisaged corridor hold political traction? High-level commitment and potential champions are critical to a successful ECD. This is even more critical for cross-border ECDs.
- Will the corridor appeal to broader constituencies such as the private sector, civil society, or international financial institutions (IFIs)?
- How large is the private sector's demand? How would the private sector visualize the development of a greenfield corridor as against investing in brownfield areas?
- What is the possible environmental impact and impact on smaller or marginalized economic actors? If negative, how can they be mitigated?
- Would the vision of the economic corridor be consistent within the macroeconomic context of the countries involved?

Stage 2: Initial stakeholder consultations and early-stage memorandum of understanding. Stakeholder consultations are important at nearly all stages. But the initial consultation is critical to assess whether the countries and their administrative regions are willing to consider the proposed

---

[32] Because each economic corridor is unique, the broad sequencing of the developments presented may vary in detail under specific contexts. The "stages" proposed here are better understood as processes rather than events at a point in time. They can often run in parallel, with relative emphasis across different stages dependent on the specifics of the corridor, including its structural contour, stakeholders involved, and the speed of progress along some dimensions.

ECD vision.[33] In a cross-country context, it is also recommended to formalize through a memorandum of understanding (MOU) between participating governments for their support in principle for the proposed ECD. The MOU can be signed by central or regional governments (with the participation of central governments) and development partners if relevant. The MOU will cite government ownership as a prerequisite to involving government agencies in subsequent ECD stages. The need for government ownership and sustained high-level political commitment has been central to the success of all large-scale ECDs. Consultations on corridor vision or proof-of-concept with selected stakeholders—such as IFIs or private associations—important to resource mobilization and ECD implementation are also useful at this stage. Including the private sector from the beginning—for example, to identify and secure connectivity involving a particular value chain or initiatives that improve the business climate—is essential in establishing an effective lobby to ensure progress and to champion the proposed ECD.

Strong government ownership is a critical prerequisite to designing a strong ECD. Aside from investments in physical infrastructure—where governments are active partners to ADB's operations—other ECD components linked to policy and market reforms, regulations and institutions would be difficult to move forward without ownership of all governments concerned. Government commitment is also necessary as ECDs, by design, focus resources on one concentrated area (as opposed to other areas) and would typically involve sensitive issues like land acquisition. An important corollary is that an ECD needs to be demand-driven to ensure government ownership. Consistency with existing national plans enhances government ownership. In addition, ECD planners should be alert to other ways governments may benefit to boost their support for ECD success. For example, as one key effect of spatial economic development is to raise land and property values, local governments have a strong incentive to promote spatial development to increase revenues via property taxes.

Stage 3: Detailed strategic feasibility study. This stage develops the proof-of-concept into a more formal and extensive strategic feasibility study. It would have to be sufficiently deep for a major ECD and would normally be financed by an IFI or major donor agency, with governments providing in-kind participation through personnel (such as early-stage working groups). The strategic feasibility study would need a detailed evaluation of existing economic and structural conditions, potential advantages and disadvantages of the targeted area, the potential for developing value chains, requirements for promoting business services and a conducive business environment, and help the countries involved negotiate an acceptable balance of differentials in costs and benefits for the ECD components for each country. Details of hardware investments and software reforms and initiatives will need to be identified without getting into detailed designs or analytics of individual investments at this stage. Sectoral strategies and spatial planning within the region will also need to be reviewed or assessed. The feasibility of mobilizing counterpart investment from the private sector would be considered, as would environmental impacts and social issues, for example, women and minorities, along with land tenure and labor mobility. As the feasibility study may take considerable time, consultations should be held with all relevant government agencies involved at different ECD milestones or phases of the study.

Stage 4a: Masterplan, project prioritization, and pipeline. The strategic feasibility study should ideally include a substantive medium-term master plan for the ECD along with a pipeline of potential projects. These preliminary plans need to be detailed and formalized in consultation with participating government entities, confirming the areas or scope of the ECD in terms of priority and sequencing of projects, reforms, and other initiatives required. Continued government ownership of the masterplan

---

[33]   A robust discussion and assessment of the existing conditions of a proposed cross-border ECD is essential at this stage. These include fragility, or closed borders due to political factors, or "thick borders" due to vested interests. Discussions and any possibility for agreement or not would be part of Stage 3, the strategic feasibility study.

should be formalized through another MOU or alternative inter-government agreement. It is also important at this stage that the ECD masterplan and project pipeline are incorporated into the development plans and investment programs of participating countries. Given the scale and scope of most ECDs, no single government or development partner can provide all the needed financial, technical, and knowledge resources. Coordination with development partners should be an integral part of this stage, though it should start as early as stages 2 and 3. Private sector consultations should begin early, especially if there are plans for PPPs and if reforms will impact private investors. Developing a high-quality masterplan and reaching an agreement with governments may take time but is essential to a successful ECD. At the same time, implementing "early harvest" or signature projects can help make the planned ECD more tangible, broadening the interest of development partners, governments, and the private sector. This would help ECDs center on a transport spine (for example, SASEC's Vizag-Chennai Industrial Corridor). However, an ECD can be successful even without a transport spine as an early harvest project, such as ABEC (Box 3).

Stage 4b: Institutional coordination mechanisms. A Zone IV ECD will have a wide range of ECD interventions requiring extensive coordination and stakeholder consultations across the government agencies of participating countries. Governments at the central, provincial, and local levels may all be involved in the discussion on institutional mechanisms covering coordination and cooperation. These will need to be formalized through inter-government agreements or MOUs along with the financing for ECD, which may initially come from IFIs with support from governments. Over time, success with an ECD can provide opportunities for incorporating the private sector into these institutions, shifting them toward partial or full cost recovery commercially. In practice, the inter-government agreement should include a supranational authority to manage the ECD. As mentioned, the design details of the supranational authority must be carefully considered.

Stage 4c: Resource mobilization, partnerships. At the same time as Stages 4a and 4b, the agreed master plan, project pipeline, and institutional mechanisms should be accompanied by resource mobilization from other stakeholders, particularly the private sector and development partners. It is important to ensure adequate financing for both investment projects and their soft components, such as institutional development and operations, capacity building, and subsequent-stage analyses (for monitoring or special purpose issues, for example).

Stage 5: Individual project development, design, and implementation. This stage begins the implementation of the master plan based on the detailed designs, funding, and priority project pipeline identified as part of the ECD.

Stage 6: Monitoring and evaluation: Given the scope of the Zone IV ECD, monitoring and evaluation should start early during implementation and continue regularly as and when needed—at both the project level and ECD level. Monitoring and evaluation provide important information for steering course corrections as needed and inputs for repeating Stages 4–6 over the longer term as the ECD continues to build momentum.

Box 3: Almaty–Bishkek Economic Corridor:
Building Momentum without "Early Harvest" Projects

The Almaty–Bishkek Economic Corridor (ABEC) was launched at the signing of a memorandum of understanding between the governments of Almaty, Kazakhstan, and Bishkek, the Kyrgyz Republic, in November 2014. A pilot economic corridor in the heart of Central Asia, ABEC is unique among Asian Development Bank (ADB)-supported corridors in that it is not based on investing in a transport spine (Almaty and Bishkek were already connected by a good transport corridor. Several years prior to ABEC). Instead, the corridor focused on the software needed to shorten the economic distance between the two cities and surrounding regions and create an integrated competitive market for health, education, and tourism, and aggregate agricultural produce in wholesale markets (https://www.almaty-bishkek.org/). Other initiatives considered included a direct bus service between Almaty and Bishkek, alternative road and rail links between the two cities, and cooperation on disaster risk reduction and urban planning.

From ABEC's inception, ADB provided technical assistance (TA) for analytical studies and for institutional coordination between the two countries. In 2017, the governments of Kazakhstan and the Kyrgyz Republic formalized the ABEC Subcommittee as the top coordinating institution. Both governments constantly interact in various ABEC sectoral working groups to strengthen regional cooperation and to develop, implement, and review investment projects and regulatory reforms. ADB TA projects have financed the preparation of regional masterplans, concepts, and pre-feasibility studies, which contributed to project concepts further refined through transaction and other knowledge and support TAs. The validation of the country partnership strategy for the Kyrgyz Republic 2018–2022 described ABEC support as groundbreaking and innovative.[a]

By 2022, 8 years since its inception, ABEC has generated a "wide web" of projects and initiatives across various sectors. ADB-supported regional investment project concepts have been approved for the development of agricultural value chains and the sustainable tourism development project in the Issyk-Kul administrative region.[b] ADB is also preparing a project to modernize border crossing points.[c] The first ABEC-supported project to modernize medical reference laboratories was approved by ADB in September 2022 for the Kyrgyz Republic.[d] Additional ABEC initiatives include preparatory legal and pre-feasibility work for an alternative road between Almaty and Issyk-Kul oblast,[e] a pre-feasibility study for the Turgen Mountain Resort,[f] and an innovative approach for deploying a high-density network of air quality sensors in Almaty and Bishkek as a baseline for air quality projects and to guide clean air action plans.[g] To promote the recovery of regional tourism following the coronavirus pandemic, ADB supported the development of a unified accommodation classification system,[h] common health and safety protocols and measures, and a business plan for a tourism skiing center in Almaty. To boost resilience against future pandemics through regional cooperation, the two countries signed an ABEC action plan to develop reference laboratories, 2022–2024 in December 2021.[i] Based on this ABEC preparatory work, the two prime ministers agreed to establish regular direct bus connections between Almaty and Bishkek using ADB-provided mobile passport scanners at border crossing points. The first direct bus connection began in August 2022.

[a] Independent Evaluation Department. 2022. *Validation of the Kyrgyz Republic Country Partnership Strategy Final Review, 2018–2022.* Manila. ADB.

[b] ADB. 2018. *Technical Assistance for Almaty–Bishkek Economic Corridor: Preparing the Modern Agriculture Wholesale Market Development Project.* Manila (TA 9677-REG). The project was planned to include wholesale market projects in Kazakhstan and the Kyrgyz Republic, but only the Kyrgyz part of the TA has been implemented to date; ADB. 2022. *Issyk-Kul Environmental Management and Sustainable Tourism Development Project.* Manila. (TRTA activities supported by TA 6819-REG).

[c] ADB. 2022. *Indicative Country Pipeline and Monitoring Report, 2023–2025.* Manila. (TRTA activities supported by TA 6819-REG).

[d] ADB. 2022. *Loan 4212-KGZ: Strengthening Regional Health Security Project. Manila (TA 6818-KGZ)* and ADB. 2018. *Assessment Report for Diagnostic and Reference Laboratory Functions in National Laboratory Systems in the Kazakhstan and Kyrgyz Republic.* Consultant's Report. Manila (Output of TA 9487-REG).

[e] ADB. 2020. *Almaty–Issyk-Kul Alternative Road Economic Impact Assessment.* Manila (Output of TA 9487-REG).

[f] ADB. 2021. *Technical Assistance to the Republic of Kazakhstan for the Pre-Feasibility Study on Turgen Mountain Resort Development.* Manila (TA 6729-KAZ).

[g] ABEC. Air Quality. (accessed on 6 September 2022) (Supported by TA 9487-REG).

[h] ADB. 2021. *Proposed Joint Accommodation Classification System for Kazakhstan and the Kyrgyz Republic. Consultant's report.* Manila (Output of TA 9487-REG).

[i] Government of Kazakhstan and Government of the Kyrgyz Republic. 2021. Action Plan for the Development of Reference Laboratories under the Economic Corridor Almaty–Bishkek for 2022–2024. Bishkek and Nur-Sultan. Unpublished.

Source: Asian Development Bank.

Crosscutting Issues

There are several important crosscutting issues relevant to designing all ECD zones. They include the role of the public sector, governance, projects, and the need to address social inclusion and environmental impact. Inadequately addressing any of these could jeopardize the feasibility and sustainability of any ECD.

Role of the Public Sector

The public sector typically has a significant role to play at the earlier stages of ECD, when the corridor is being planned and designed. The government is also likely to play a leading role in certain aspects of an ECD if the geographical region has a large population or is cross-border. Ensuring that the public sector of participating countries has adequate technical and decision-making capacities needs to be part of the ECD. There are five areas where the government will need to be active: (i) as ECD champion and signaling long-term commitment—with major corridor development taking even decades to complete, high-level government commitment provides the needed credibility and confidence for investors and helps address differences in stakeholders' opinion; (ii) as a primary provider of basic infrastructure and, over time, as catalyst and facilitator for private infrastructure services; (iii) as a provider of a good business environment (including macro stability); (iv) in providing oversight and managing and monitoring public goods, including social and environmental impact; and (v) as an institutional coordinator between the many entities involved, such as different tiers of government and various line ministries and agencies from each country involved, as well as the private sector and civil society stakeholders.

Governments have additional critical roles to play in Zone IV ECDs. They will need to lead negotiations and implement cross-border policy coordination and harmonization. More complex—but equally critical to success—is the role played by government in (i) negotiating the distribution of positive cross-border spillovers of public goods and regional benefits—these may need to be distributed equitably rather than equally, and conversely; (ii) addressing any negative externalities that must be mitigated and managed through the collective action of participating countries.

Governance

No matter how well an ECD may be designed, good governance in its institutional mechanisms is a prerequisite to success and sustainability. Weak political and economic governance is a barrier to domestic and foreign investment. A major ECD involves the commitment of large public sector resources that can have different effects across the regions and industries within the corridor. The corridor will typically include a multitude of stakeholders with diverse interests—across countries, different tiers of government, private entities, social groups, and political coalitions. Without well-functioning institutions and good governance, it will be difficult to negotiate the inevitable trade-offs and sustain the ECD over the long term. The ECD, therefore, needs to negotiate and build into its design mechanisms for transparency, multi-stakeholder participation, and accountability in its institutions to ensure predictable decision-making through the consistent application of the rules, regulations, and laws of the countries involved.

Social Inclusion and Environmental Impact

The scope and scale of any ambitious ECD—in terms of infrastructure investments and policy and institutional reforms—can have substantial and asymmetric effects on society. For long-term social welfare and ECD sustainability, planners and designers must include vulnerable social groups and prevent the elite from capturing the benefits of the corridor. Maintaining cross-border inclusiveness and convergence is particularly important in ensuring the long-term sustainability of cross-border corridors. For example, cross-border community cooperation initiatives targeting disadvantaged groups, such as small-scale cross-border traders, can help address these issues. Similarly, careful monitoring of the environmental impact of investments and planning for economic transformation needs to be part of the ECD to ensure that adequate preventive, mitigative, and adaptive actions are implemented as necessary.

Success Factors and Potential Pitfalls

Even a modest ECD will likely involve a significant commitment of financial resources, policy reforms that benefit some stakeholders but not all, and social and environmental impact. Experience has also shown that an ECD can take years to develop—the three corridors reviewed in chapter III took more than a decade from conceptualization into implementation. Having designed, initiated, and begun implementation, how can planners, government officials, and other stakeholders assess the success of an ECD? What are the key performance criteria that should be used as "guard rails" as an ECD progresses? In discussing specific performance indicators, it is worth noting that assessing some success factors will partly overlap with monitoring and evaluation, particularly at the project level, and that some assessments may be technically demanding in terms of the data needed and attributing impact to the ECD. There are at least three categories of determinants of success: economic, social, and RPGs, such as environmental impact.

Economic performance criteria will obviously depend upon the ECD objectives—for example, job creation, export promotion, regional value chain development, growth, spatial decentralization, or targeted sectors such as tourism, biotech, or agriculture, to mention a few. Some regional-level macroeconomic indicators will likely be common across most ECDs, such as growth in regional GDP, the quantity and quality of jobs created, private investment generated—particularly foreign direct investment—and the contribution to net exports.[34] Ideally, it would be useful to scale these indicators by the amount of resources invested in the ECD to determine the outcome per unit invested.

Social indicators are important within the broad spectrum of ECD. Given the scale of resources invested and the different impacts of policy and institutional interventions, it is important to examine key social indicators such as poverty and inequality across the corridor area (by income and other measures), the economic status of socially vulnerable and marginalized groups such as women, children, and the elderly; the status of micro-, small- and medium-sized enterprises; and the socioeconomic status of marginal and small landholders.

Large infrastructure investments underline the need for carefully monitoring the environmental impact of an ECD. The negative environmental growth impact (as traditionally measured) is a well-known empirical reality. Thus, the economic success of ECD depends on monitoring environmental indicators

---

[34] Some indicators may have intermediate indicators given the long ECD timelines, for example, the number of inquiries from domestic and private investors or new firms. Intermediate indicators are not discussed here.

specific to the attributes of the corridor area. Other RPGs (such as health, trafficking, and crime) should also be carefully monitored in assessing ECD performance.

One ECD benefit is enhanced institutional capacity of all levels of the government and improved governance. Where relevant and feasible, these indicators of ECD performance can also be useful to monitor.

Some potential pitfalls in ECD implementation that require careful attention were noted in the empirical review in chapters IV and V. These include (i) lack of adequate institutional structures, either due to absence of a supra-regional corridor authority or design weaknesses; (ii) ability of vested interests to continue corrupt practices; (iii) poor coordination among multiple stakeholders; (iv) lack of consensus among different governments and their agencies; and (v) project implementation issues over land acquisition and clearances, among others. Corridor performance should be frequently assessed against the progress and success of these institutional dimensions. Providing last-mile infrastructure services and the availability of an adequate skilled workforce can also be overlooked.

There are two other important potential pitfalls that are broad in category and frequent in practice. The first is improper design due to political interference or poor technical and economic analysis. It is critical to avoid choosing areas that lack intrinsic potential or have limited benefits relative to resources committed or those that are chosen for political or non-economic purposes. Targeting industries or sectors must be free from political interference or poor technical and economic analysis. More generally, designing an ECD that is inconsistent with the area's initial conditions will likely result in poor technical preparation.

The other pitfall to avoid is assuming adequate resources can be mobilized, particularly on the private capital to be attracted from domestic or foreign sources. Experience has shown that the private capital attracted often falls short of projections and targets. Over-optimistic assumptions and projections are often made about PPPs that are incompatible with the legal and regulatory environment within the corridor area, the availability of public and private capital, and the government's overall investment priorities. Another factor to monitor is whether and to what extent the corridor is "crowding in" private and public investment. An ECD should augment existing investments within the corridor area and beyond.

7 Mainstreaming Economic Corridor Development into ADB Operations

ADB needs to innovate and take a stronger approach to economic corridor development.
Technically complex, multisector and multi-stakeholder, ECD requires large preparatory and investment resources to be an effective development or investment tool. An economic corridor typically has a long gestation period and lag time between its initial concept and project implementation. It can strain annual quantitative targets for approvals and disbursements. In over two decades of ECD in subregional programs, ADB's focus has been primarily on Zone I transport corridors, with some work on Zone II cross-border transport corridors. Initiatives over the past 5 years show a welcome shift toward S-type Zone III and IV corridors or ECD. These include SASEC's Vizag-Chennai Industrial Corridor and other recently approved projects, along with CAREC's ABEC and potentially STKEC programs. While GMS has begun several urban development projects in some towns along its transport corridors, there is no integrated ECD masterplan. ECD plans in GMS still focus on activities and potential "along" corridors to "transform" them into economic corridors. Overall, subregional programs remain characterized by operating in sector silos with limited coordination across sectors. ADB needs to adopt a bolder approach to ECD.

Strategy 2030 outlines new opportunities for economic corridor development. ADB's New Operating Model (NOM)[35] will help better implement Strategy 2030 and next-generation economic corridors by integrating all sectors under a single sectors group. There are specific organizational and structural factors that can help determine how ADB can lead in developing the new generation of S-type corridors or economic corridors. How can these new initiatives be mainstreamed into ADB's RCI operations?[36]

Why should ADB undertake economic corridor development, given its complexity, resource requirements, and lengthy-time horizon? A strong rationale is the potential impact—nationally, regionally, and even globally—that has increased demand for ECD from DMCs. India, Malaysia, the PRC, and Thailand are actively pursuing ECD.[37] However, many lower-income economies lack the technical, financial, and administrative capacity to design, develop and implement economic corridors by themselves. ECD initiatives should ensure that ADB and government efforts do not overlap private sector investment in corridor development. ADB should limit its interventions to those with a clear public sector role. In middle-income economies with a robust, expanding private sector, private investment and PPPs will play a greater role in ECD. But in lower-income countries, where markets and the private sector are less developed, the need for government action with ADB assistance may be larger.

---

[35] ADB's New Operating Model (NOM) was launched on 30 June 2023, to be fully operational by 2025.
[36] The discussion and suggestions related to the organizational aspects of ADB and mainstreaming ECD remain to be tested and adjusted within the recently adopted NOM.
[37] There continues to be much discussion over ECD in other countries as part of their regional and sector development plans.

A second rationale is that ECD allows ADB to "stress test" its evolving "One-ADB approach" through ECD. An important challenge will be to design more integrated multisector programs on a subnational and/or regional scale. The challenges faced by DMCs increasingly require S-type solutions, such as urbanization and economic diversification. ADB requires more experience with spatial, multisector programs that can better help DMCs tackle future challenges as they continue to move into higher income levels.[38]

ADB's strength in economic corridor development starts with its expertise and experience in physical infrastructure. ADB has several advantages in undertaking the new generation of ECD. First is its comparative advantage, expertise, and knowledge in designing and implementing hard infrastructure projects, which would dominate the early phases of ECD. ADB's success in developing regional transport corridors, as well as in power, agriculture, and urban development, attests to this advantage.[39] Lately, RCI operations have also succeeded in addressing soft infrastructure, such as introducing single windows for customs clearance as part of TTF and measures in response to the COVID-19 pandemic.

ADB's role as an honest broker and portfolio manager is critical for multi-stakeholder programs. With its experience and credibility, ADB has strong convening power for bringing together the diverse stakeholders needed for next-generation ECD. ADB's RCI programs have demonstrated expertise in coordinating across countries, sectors, and stakeholders, including development partners and the private sector.

Availability and ability to mobilize financial resources. ADB has the financial and technical resources to help governments plan ECD, including early technical and economic analysis along with consultations with governments, stakeholders, and in building institutions. ADB's constant contact with development partners in RCI operations can help mobilize additional financial, technical, and knowledge resources.

ADB's array of financing tools can be customized to the needs of economic corridor development. ADB has a wide range of financing options or instruments available for ECD. Experience suggests that the appropriate financial modality will depend on the specific country and regional circumstances. In countries with shallow financial markets, weak regulatory frameworks, and difficult land acquisition issues, corridor projects would largely depend on financing by governments and development partners. Harnessing PPPs tend to be easier for national rather than cross-border projects, which are bundled with political, social, and economic risks. In these instances, extending guarantees can play a significant facilitating role. Financing options also depend on the corridor elements being developed. In earlier stages, for example, ADB's technical assistance would play an important role in supporting institutional coordination along with analytical and technical preparatory work. Policy and institutional reforms in an ECD package can be supported by program lending or results-based lending. ADB sector-development finance would be essential in areas or sectors where physical infrastructure investments must be combined with policy reforms. Regular infrastructure investments are usually financed by the public sector, development banks, or PPPs. However, investments in urban corridor development may require greater private sector financing. This is particularly true as corridors reach more advanced stages of development, given the use of more ADB private sector instruments for ECD.

---

[38] With some notable exceptions, such as joint teams between the PSOD and regional departments for nonsovereign state-owned operations, or ADB's pandemic response, multisector ECD operations would be on a different scale.

[39] Zone I corridors remain relevant for many parts of Asia and the Pacific and should remain a priority for RCI operations. But after more than 2 decades of RCI and ECD, opportunities and demand for Zone I corridors will likely continue to decline. Nonetheless, the role of Zone I corridors as a first phase of S-type ECD remains large.

Soft infrastructure or software remains weak. ECD requires much soft infrastructure or "software," such as policy, market, and institutional reform. ADB's experience in this RCI area has been only partially successful. Zone II corridors have long been part of ADB's RCI programs, but their success remains elusive. Software is intrinsically more difficult than hard infrastructure. There are also some structural constraints and organizational issues internal to ADB. Experience with software offers lessons on some issues relevant to ADB mainstreaming next generation ECD. These include fragmented working arrangements, aligning responsibilities and accountability, and the role played by quantitative analysis and targeting.

Fragmented organizational arrangements need to be unified. For example, prior to NOM, TTF operations were organized differently across ADB-supported three subregional programs. In GMS, TTF has at times been in the regional cooperation and operations coordination division, later in the public sector management, finance, and trade division, of SERD. In CAREC, both EARD and CWRD handle TTF projects. However, in EARD, TTF projects are handled by the public sector management, finance, and trade division, which has a partial function of the CAREC secretariat (on trade sector work), while in CWRD, the regional cooperation and operations coordination division which serves as the CAREC secretariat, has no mandate for project processing, resulting in TTF investment projects being developed, designed, and implemented in other divisions instead. In contrast to SASEC, TTF projects are handled entirely within the regional cooperation and operations coordination division of SARD. These fragmented organizational arrangements for TTF can dilute coordination and effectiveness and, therefore should be unified.

Lessons from TTF for mainstreaming economic corridor development. Software components of an S-type corridor or economic corridor involve much more than TTF. Lessons from TTF operations would suggest ensuring there is a less fragmented organizational ECD structure, along with clearer targeting, responsibility, and rewards for relevant teams. A wider set of software issues would also come with substantive resource utilization for broader and more robust project pipelines integral to Zone III and Zone IV ECDs. This may facilitate greater focus from concerned departments on prioritizing ECD hardware and software together.

Software work adds little to annual operational targets. In addition to being intrinsically harder to implement, software projects are also less resource intensive than hardware projects. This obviously affects the regional departments' incentives that face quantitative targets for project approvals, commitments, and disbursements. This results in greater management attention paid to infrastructure projects requiring larger investments.

Software is difficult for both managers and staff. The greater implementation challenge and longer timeline of software projects also muddies targets and objectives for operational staff. This limits accountability and also dilutes appreciation and rewards from management for project processing staff.[40]

There should be sustained commitment at the highest level of government with a long-term perspective. For countries doing ECD, there must be sustained commitment at the highest level, a long-term perspective, and mechanisms to ensure coordination across multiple stakeholders. This is true for ADB as well. Under the NOM, regional departments, sector groups, and country management teams led by the respective director generals must be fully committed to any ECD initiative, including a clear understanding of the gestation lag between conceptualization and the various stages of ECD before a project starts.

---

[40]   The GMS CBTA, for example, has been under implementation for over 20 years and is still seeking "early harvests." It would thus be difficult to assess staff contributions to the success or remaining CBTA issues.

Dedicated economic corridor development operations team. A dedicated ECD team or unit needs to be established with clear reporting lines, responsibilities, and accountability to ensure efficient multisector hardware and software coordination. The size of the core team would depend upon a corridor's scope and stage of development, with greater needs in the stages before a masterplan is finalized and project implementation starts. Given these technical requirements, the core team should be led by a senior international staff (at least Level 6) with demonstrated technical skills and supported by at least two other international staff. Prior to NOM, existing subregional programs were mostly sector driven, with sector divisions undertaking silo-based subregional strategies, programming, and projects. Coordination across sectors is the responsibility of the regional cooperation and operations coordination divisions, but an integrated multisector economic corridor would require much stronger coordination. Unlike sector teams, regional cooperation and operations coordination divisions are mostly confined to secretariat roles without processing mandates.

The economic corridor development team requires diversified skills and should include resident mission support. The core ECD operational team would need to combine both project processing and coordination skills with expertise in multiple sectors. Specifically, the team should have (i) deep familiarity with regional perspectives, diagnostics, and planning with active policy dialogue skills; (ii) experience with multi-country, multi-sector, and multi-stakeholder projects, and a strong ability to manage multi-sector frameworks; (iii) abilities for institutional coordination across multiple government and nongovernment agencies; and (iv) a good track record in resource mobilization. Additional team members may be drawn from different divisions and departments with specialized task-based consultants with clear responsibility, accountability, and reporting lines. An ECD team cannot coordinate effectively without strong departmental management support. To ensure ECD operations are integrated into ADB's programming cycle, the operations team will need to include resident mission staff in handling country programming and strategy. Heads of the project administration unit in the resident missions should also be part of the ECD team, given the increasing delegation of project implementation to resident missions.

Location of the economic corridor development team. The location of the ECD operational team within ADB is critical. One option can be an organizationally centralized place with deep regional and operational familiarity and the ability to handle multiple ECD initiatives across different regions and sectors. The ECD team will be supported by ECD focal points from the regional departments (e.g., RCI Unit) and the Sectors Group. This institutional setup for ECD would have the advantage of improved coordination across regions and sectors, better access to department management, greater oversight, accountability, and rewards for staff incentives.

The Finance Sector Office can play a useful role in economic corridor development. Finance divisions under the Finance Sector Office (SG-FIN) can be expanded to play a major role in RCI, particularly in relation to ECD. The divisions' core competences are industry and trade, SME development, finance, public financial management, and PPPs—all critically needed for ECD. Moreover, the finance divisions are well-versed in project preparation and implementation, particularly in utilizing lending modalities other than project loans, such as policy-based lending, result-based lending, multitranche financing facility (MFF), financial institutions loans, and nonlending modalities including guarantees and risk participation. The finance divisions could also be in a good position to selectively provide mission leadership while assembling multisector and multi-thematic mission teams.

The link between subregional programs and ECD. It is likely that ECD operations will grow considerably in size and scope over time, potentially becoming a "program within the subregional program." Considering the potential overlap, ECD initiatives will be distinct from subregional programs. RCI units need to reorient to fully incorporate ECD operations into their reporting mechanism (e.g., at ministerial, senior official, and expert group meetings under subregional programs), as well as for analytical work covering sector, thematic, institutional, and broader program strategies. The ECD master plan and its project pipeline need to be an integral part of the subregional program's strategy, implementation plans, and results framework.[41]

Role of the Office of Markets Development and Public–Private Partnership and the Private Sector Operations Department. The development and implementation of ECD projects increasingly involve private sector participation. Private sector participation in designing an ECD masterplan should be an important objective that could require a more active role for the Office of Markets Development and Public–Private Partnership (OMDP) and PSOD. It would be important to consider including OMDP at the ECD planning stage to explore opportunities for private sector participation and to stimulate the private sector's interest. Later, during implementation, involving PSOD should be considered to show ADB's commitment to bringing together sovereign and nonsovereign funding. PSOD also uses many financing tools, from equity, funds, and loans, to nonfunded programs such as guarantees and risk participation. These tools can also be combined with sovereign financing instruments used to match client needs for ECD.

Knowledge work is continuous across the economic corridor development stages. The One-ADB approach to ECD also means knowledge departments such as the Economic Research and Development Impact Department (ERDI), the Climate Change and Sustainable Development Department (CCSD), and the ADB Institute need to work closely with ECD teams. The ECD framework requires extensive knowledge and analytical work at the planning stages as well as during implementation and evaluation.

The link between Thematic Groups and economic corridor development. The Regional Cooperation and Integration and Trade Division (CCRC) under CCSD provides policy, technical, and funding support for ADB-wide RCI operations and links RCI-related units and communities across ADB. The CCRC can work with RCI units of regional departments and the Sectors Group on the lessons learned from existing and completed ECD projects, prepare case studies; produce tool kits, and facilitate data collection and reporting. It can also liaise with the Strategy, Policy, and Partnerships Department on drafting and updating the guidance note and later staff instructions or operations manual as needed. Other thematic groups also have expertise and interests in ECD, such as in health, climate change, and disaster risk management, as RPGs. The SG-FIN can be involved in cross-border financial services and fintech applications, including SME finance. To coordinate the various groups in CCSD, the CCRC can coordinate ECD teams so they are aware of CCSD's latest work and connect with experts as required.

Multitranche financing facilities can be used for economic corridor development. The MFF is a suitable loan structure for ECD as it can properly sequence multiple project components under a single loan for ECD projects. It is flexible in adjusting project components and the composition of project teams to meet changing needs when early tranches are being implemented and later tranches are being prepared. MFFs also show strong ADB borrower commitment to comprehensive and long-term ECD.

Working with development partners to cofinance economic corridor development. Outside ADB, resource mobilization is also an ECD challenge. Zone IV economic corridors would normally be a longer-term objective for RCI operations. But a Zone III corridor may be a prerequisite stage—along with a Zone II corridor. Resource mobilization will be more difficult unless other development partners

---

[41]   All ECD projects financed by ADB would naturally go through ADB's programming cycle. This would raise a host of issues related to requirements for ensuring high-quality project preparation, design, implementation, and evaluation. These project-level issues are not considered here as they are similar for all ADB projects, whether or not they are part of an ECD initiative.

agree with the new ECD framework, as they did earlier with transport corridors. ADB's consistent advocacy for the new ECD framework would be a necessary first step given ADB's leadership in RCI.

Selectivity in launching economic corridor development. Much as the concept of an economic corridor rests on focusing efforts and resources in a targeted area, RCI operations need to be selective when it comes to ECD. Instead of spreading resources thinly across several corridors, the focus should be on choosing a few ECDs with high potential development impact at any given time. A ceiling of two or three per region would already be generous. A few successful programs would provide good examples for others considering ECD.

Pressure for a quick project to meet quantitative targets should be avoided at early economic corridor development stages. The sequencing of ECD is also important. Compared with one-off infrastructure projects, ECD is more capital-intensive, with longer gestation lags and higher returns over time (in terms of a deep project pipeline and higher development impact). The initial ECD phases need to be insulated from the pressure of "quarterly returns" or immediate project identification and implementation. ECD should be initiated only with the knowledge that early projects will be operational only after 18–24 months, during which TA resources will be used for comprehensive consultations, masterplan development, and institutional and capacity strengthening.

Small steps can bring big returns. ADB can accumulate additional experience in the early stages by attaching sector projects in pipelines. Specifically, S-type corridor or ECD practitioners can consolidate sector projects that focus on an identified region to explore ECD in partnership with government(s). These could be relatively modest by geographical scale and scope, such as developing a FEA anchored on a GMS corridor town, for example, or a small-scale domestic agglomeration such as Tashkent-Samarkand or Dushanbe-Kurgon Teppe in CAREC.

Initiate and strengthen work with development partners on the new economic corridor development approach. Preliminary feedback from development partners in preparation for this guidance note showed strong support for the new ECD approach. It came with a desire for (i) wider dissemination and dialogue among more partners to build a shared understanding of the proposed ECD approach and identify good practices for improved coordination among partners, and (ii) co-organizing roundtables and similar events on the new ECD approach for a more focused dialogue between development partners actively engaged in ECD.

APPENDIX 1
Map of Greater Mekong Subregion Economic Corridors

GREATER MEKONG SUBREGION

Configuration of Greater Mekong Subregion Economic Corridors

Legend

★ National Capital
• City and Town
—— North–South Economic Corridor
—— Southern Economic Corridor
—— East–West Economic Corridor
- - - East–West Potential Extension
- - - Provincial Boundary
- - - International Boundary

N

0   500
Kilometers

This map was produced by the cartography unit of the Asian Development Bank. The boundaries, colors, denominations, and any other information shown on this map do not imply, on the part of the Asian Development Bank, any judgement on the legal status of any territory, or any other endorsement or acceptance of such boundaries, colors, denominations, or information.

Source: Asian Development Bank.

Map of the Central Asia Regional Economic Cooperation Economic Corridors

Almaty–Bishkek Economic Corridor

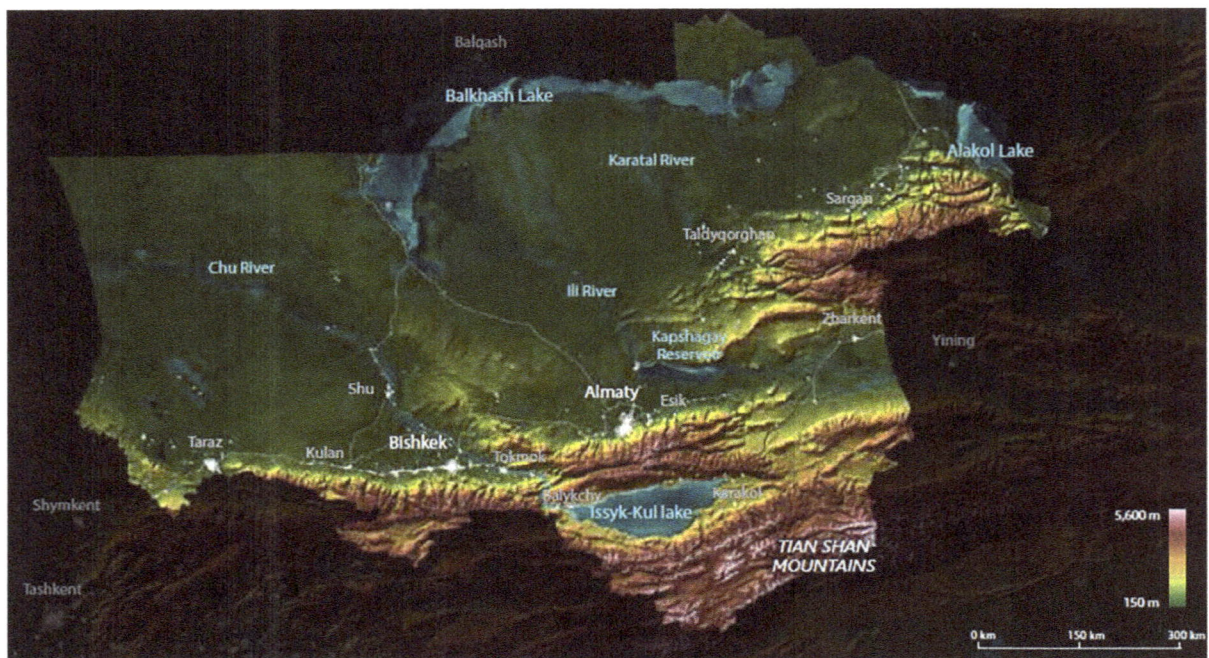

Source: DIVA-GIS. http:www.diva-gis.org/.

Shymkent–Tashkent–Khujand Economic Corridors

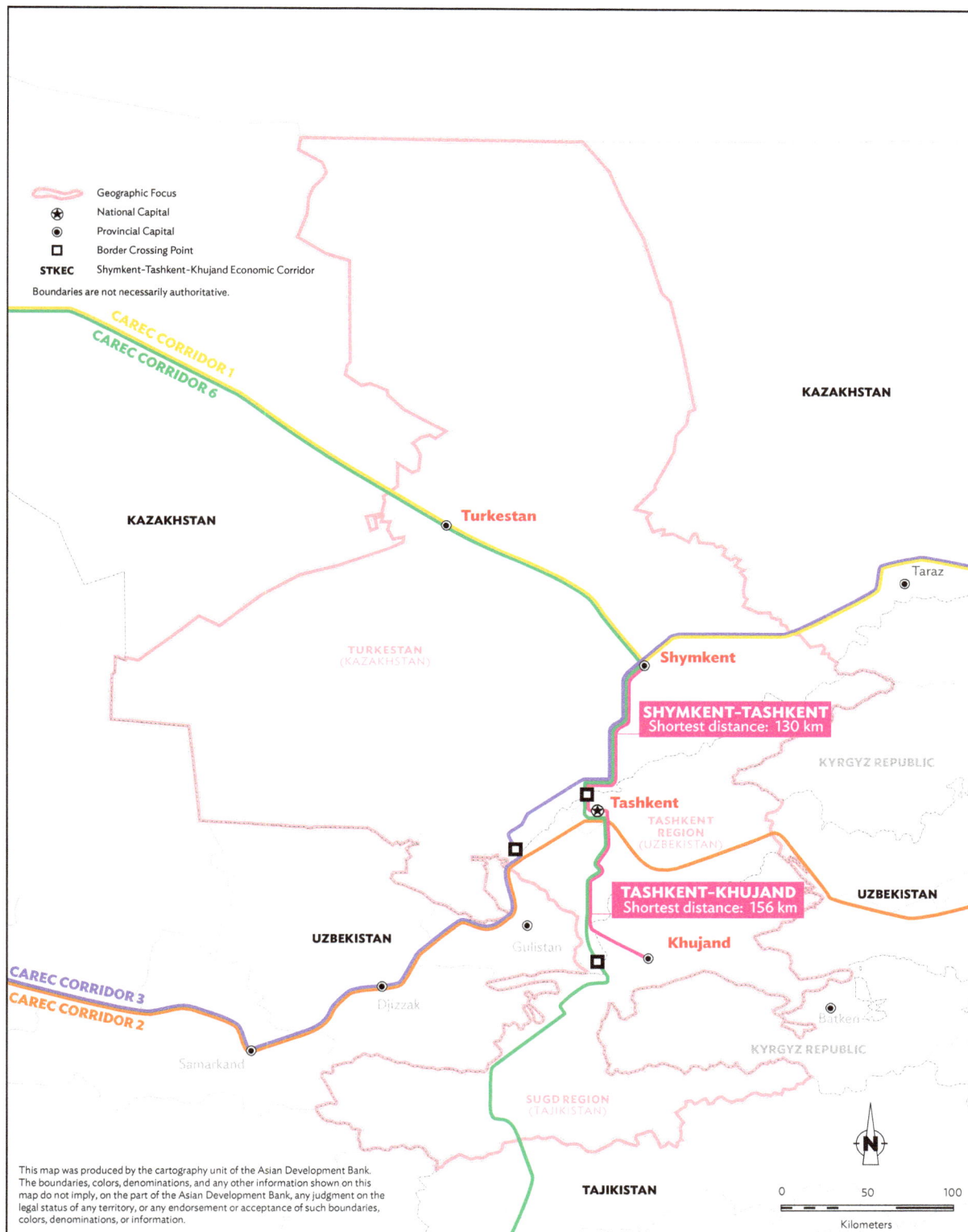

Legend:
- Geographic Focus
- National Capital
- Provincial Capital
- Border Crossing Point
- STKEC — Shymkent-Tashkent-Khujand Economic Corridor

Boundaries are not necessarily authoritative.

CAREC CORRIDOR 1
CAREC CORRIDOR 6

KAZAKHSTAN

KAZAKHSTAN

Turkestan

Taraz

TURKESTAN
(KAZAKHSTAN)

Shymkent

SHYMKENT–TASHKENT
Shortest distance: 130 km

KYRGYZ REPUBLIC

Tashkent

TASHKENT
REGION
(UZBEKISTAN)

TASHKENT–KHUJAND
Shortest distance: 156 km

UZBEKISTAN

Khujand

UZBEKISTAN

Gulistan

CAREC CORRIDOR 3
CAREC CORRIDOR 2

Djizzak

Batken

KYRGYZ REPUBLIC

Samarkand

SUGD REGION
(TAJIKISTAN)

This map was produced by the cartography unit of the Asian Development Bank.
The boundaries, colors, denominations, and any other information shown on this
map do not imply, on the part of the Asian Development Bank, any judgment on the
legal status of any territory, or any endorsement or acceptance of such boundaries,
colors, denominations, or information.

TAJIKISTAN

N

0   50   100

Kilometers

Source: Asian Development Bank.

Map of the South Asia Subregional Economic Cooperation Economic Corridors

SASEC Economic Corridors

SASEC Economic Corridors

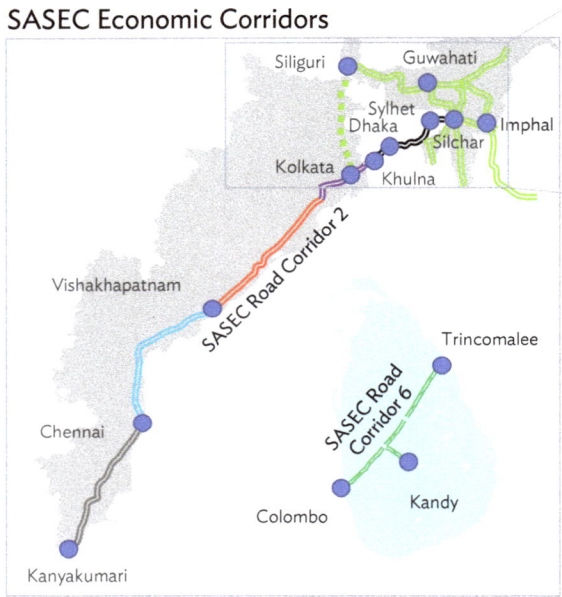

SASEC Road Corridors

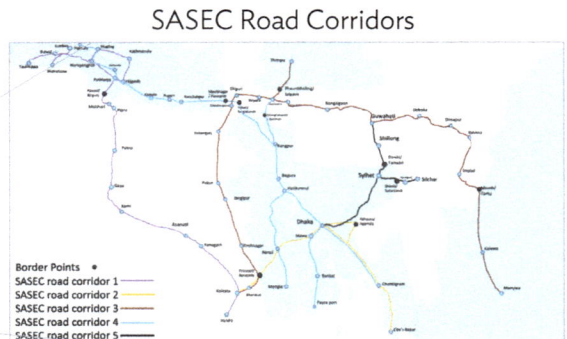

SASEC Economic Corridors

CKIC: Chennai-Kanyakumari Industrial Corridor

VCIC: Vizag-Chennai Industrial Corridor

OEC: Odisha Economic Corridor

WBEC: West Bengal Economic Corridor

NEEC: North-East Economic Corridor

Bangladesh Economic Corridor

Sri Lanka Economic Corridor

Source: Asian Development Bank.

References

ADB. 2006. *Regional Cooperation and Integration Strategy*. Manila.

———. 2014. *Operationalizing Economic Corridors in Central Asia: A Case Study of the Almaty–Bishkek Corridor*. Manila.

———. 2016. *Scaling new heights: Vizag-Chennai Industrial Corridor, India's First Coastal Corridor*. Manila.

———. 2016b. *South Asia Subregional Economic Cooperation Operational Plan 2016–2025*. Manila.

———. 2018. *Review of the Configuration of the GMS Economic Corridors*. Manila.

———. 2019. *Strategy 2030 Operational Plan for Priority 7 – Fostering Regional Cooperation and Integration, 2019–2024*. Manila.

———. 2021. *Greater Mekong Subregion Economic Cooperation Program Strategic Framework 2030*. Manila.

———. 2021. *A Roadmap for Shymkent–Tashkent–Khujand Economic Corridor*. Manila.

———. 2022. *Regional Cooperation and Integration Corporate Progress Report 2017–2020*, Manila.

Asian Development Bank, Department for International Development, Japan International Cooperation Agency, and the World Bank. 2018. *The WEB of Transport Corridors in South Asia*. Washington, DC.: World Bank.

Arnold, J. 2005. *Best Practices in Corridor Management. Report prepared for the World Bank*. Washington, DC: International Bank for Reconstruction and Development.

Arvis, Jean-Francois Arvis, Graham Smith, and Robin Carruthers (ed.) 2011. *Connecting Landlocked Developing Countries to Markets – Trade corridors in the 21st century*. Washington, DC: World Bank.

Athukorala, Prema-chandra, and Suresh Narayanan. 2017. Economic Corridors and Regional Development: The Malaysian Experience. *ADB Economics Working Paper Series* No. 520. Manila: Asian Development Bank.

Böttcher, Boris. 2006. *The Trans-European Network: History, Progress and Financing*. https://komunikacie. uniza.sk/pdfs/csl/2006/01/12.pdf.

Brand, Andrew. 2017. The use of corridor development as a strategic and supporting instrument towards the development of national space economies. Unpublished Ph.D. Thesis. Potchefstroom: North West University, South Africa.

Brunner, Hans-Peter. 2013. What is Economic Corridor Development and What Can It Achieve in Asia's Subregions? *Working Paper on Regional Economic Integration* No. 117. Manila: Asian Development Bank.

Buiter, Willem, and Ebrahim Rahbari. 2011. *Trade Transformed – The Emerging New Corridors of Trade Power.* Citi GPS: Global Perspectives & Solutions.

CAREC. 2017. *CAREC 2030: Connecting the Region for Shared and Sustainable Development.* Manila: Asian Development Bank.

Donaldson, Dave. 2010. Railways of the Raj: Estimating the Impact of Transport Infrastructure. *NBER Working Paper.* 16487. October. Cambridge, United States.

Economic Modeling Specialists Inc. 2007. *Defining a Functional Economic Region.* https://www.economicmodeling.com/wp-content/uploads/2007/10/wp_defining_functional_economic_region.pdf.

Fang, Chuanglin, and Danlin Yu. 2017. Urban Agglomeration: An Evolving Concept of An Emerging Phenomenon. *Landscape and Urban Planning.* 162 (June). pp. 126–136.

Food and Agriculture Organization. 2017. *Territorial Tools for Agro-Industry Development – A Sourcebook.* Rome.

Isono, Ikumo, and Satoru Kumagai. 2020. (Re)Defining Economic Corridors. *Discussion Paper* 774. Tokyo: Institute for Developing Economies.

Krugman, Paul. 1993. First Nature, Second Nature, and Metropolitan Location. *Regional Science.* 33(2). May.

McKinsey. 2019. *Globalization in Transition: The Future of Trade and Value Chains.* McKinsey Global Institute. January.

Roberts, Mark , Martin Melecky, Théophile Bougna, and Yan (Sarah) Xu. 2018. Transport Corridors and Their Wider Economic Benefits: A Critical Review of the Literature. *Policy Research Working Paper.* No. 8302. Washington, DC: World Bank.

Rosbach, Kristian. 2019. Testing the 3D Approach to Economic Corridor Development in Central Asia. *Asian Development Blog.* 6 February. https://blogs.adb.org/blog/testing-3d-approach-economic-corridor-development-central-asia.

Srivastava, Pradeep. 2013. Regional Corridors Development: A Framework. *Journal of International Commerce, Economics and Policy.* 4(2).

———. 2016. Spatial RCI: *Putting "Region" Back in Regional Cooperation.* mimeo. Asian Development Bank.

Sugiyarto, Guntur. 2020. *Economic Corridor Development Framework: Towards Mainstreaming Economic Corridor for Development Intervention and Investment.* mimeo. Manila: Asian Development Bank.

Sugiyarto, Guntur, and Dewan Mushtaq. 2021. *Economic Corridor Development.* mimeo. Manila: Asian Development Bank.

World Bank. 2009. *World Development Report 2009: Reshaping Economic Geography.* Washington, DC; World Bank.